BUILDINGS
and LANDMARKS
of OLD BOSTON

BUILDINGS
and LANDMARKS
of OLD BOSTON

A Guide to the Colonial, Provincial,

Federal, and Greek Revival Periods,

1630–1850

HOWARD S. ANDROS

with illustrations by the author

University Press of New England

HANOVER AND LONDON

University Press of New England, Hanover, NH 03755

© 2001 by Howard S. Andros

Printed in the United States of America

5 4 3 2 1

LIBRARY OF CONGRESS CATALOGING-IN-PUBLICATION DATA

Andros, Howard S.
  Buildings and landmarks of old Boston : a guide to the Colonial,
Provincial, Federal, and Greek Revival periods, 1630–1850 / by Howard S.
Andros ; with illustrations by the author.
    p. cm.
Includes bibliographical references.
  ISBN 1–58465–092–3 (pbk. : alk. paper)
    1. Architecture—Massachusetts—Boston—Guidebooks.   2. Historic
buildings—Massachusetts—Boston—Guidebooks. 3. Boston
(Mass.)—Guidebooks. 4. Boston (Mass.)—Buildings, structures,
etc.—Guidebooks. I. Title.
  NA735.B7 A53 2001
  720'.9744'61—dc21   2001001361

To my four children

Medford

The Provincial
Powderhouse

Somerville

Cambridge

Brookline

Revere

Everett

Chelsea   Chelsea Creek

Charlestown
Bunker Hill Mon.
the frigate Constitution

East
Boston

Winthrop

MASSACHUSETTS
BAY

The Old
Hub

Charles River

BOSTON

Roxbury

Dorchester
Heights

Shirley Place
Jamaica Plain

Jamaica Pond

Milton

Airport

Pt. Shirley

Deer I.

South Boston

Castle I.

BOSTON
HARBOR

Spectacle I.

Gallups I.

Long I.

Rainsford I.

O Green I.

Calf I.

Lovell I.   O Outer Brewster I.
                   O Middle Brewster I.
Great Brewster I. O Little Brewster I.
                   Boston Lighthouse

George's I.

Thompson I.

Dorchester
Bay

Moon I.

Squantum

Neponset River

Quincy
Bay

Hull

Peddock's I.

Sheep I.

Bumpkin I.

Hog I.

Pt. Allerton

Nantasket Beach

Grape I. Hingham Bay

Slate I.

Nantasket

Hough's
Neck

Quincy

Weymouth Fore R.

Weymouth Back R.

Hingham

Howard S. au
1980

Braintree

Weymouth

BOSTON HARBOR
Circa 1975

Contents

Colonial Period (1630–1691)

Provincial Period (1691–1783)

Federal Period (1783–circa 1820)

Greek Revival Period (circa 1820–1850)

Illustrations

Colonial Period

Provincial Period

Federal Period

Greek Revival Period

Preface

In 1920, as a thirteen-year-old office boy employed by the *Boston Evening Transcript*, I often spent my lunchtimes in a marketplace rich with patina and the blended fragrances of spices, coffees, vegetables, and fruits. There I marveled at the brawn of white-coated meat handlers shouldering great sides of beef with apparent ease. And there, if one was attentive, the clatter of draft horses on granite-block pavements and the gentle "gee and haw" of lorry drivers could still be heard above the thumping of motor trucks riding on solid rubber tires. Along the waterfront nearby, fishermen regularly unloaded their catch from Georges Bank, and, if I showed interest, they would sometimes toss me a cod "to take home to Mama." (Of course it would be wrapped in an early-afternoon edition of the *Transcript!*)

June 2000   H.S.A.

BOSTON

COLONIAL PERIOD

A-1 Boston Common
A-2 King's Chapel Burial Ground
A-3 Old Granary Burial Ground
A-4 Copp's Hill
A-5 Province Steps and Gateway
A-6 Paul Revere House

PROVINCIAL PERIOD

B-1 Capen House
B-2 Long Wharf
B-3 Moses Pierce-Hichborn House
B-4 Old Corner Bookstore
B-5 Clough House
B-6 Old State House
B-7 Christ Church
B-8 Old South Meeting House
B-9 Boston Stone
B-10 Faneuil Hall
B-11 King's Chapel
B-12 Ebenezer Hancock House
B-13 Liberty Tree

FEDERAL PERIOD

C-1 New State House
C-2 First Harrison Gray Otis House
C-3 Second Harrison Gray Otis House
C-4 14 Walnut Street
C-5 Saint Stephen's Church
C-6 Amory-Ticknor House
C-7 Nichols House
C-8 Higginson House
C-9 Third Harrison Gray Otis House
C-10 Charles Street Meeting House
C-11 54 and 55 Beacon Street
C-12 Hancock Street
C-13 West Church
C-14 Park Street Church

GREEK REVIVAL PERIOD

D-1 David Sears House
D-2 Saint Paul's Cathedral
D-3 Massachusetts General Hospital
D-4 Quincy Market
D-5 Granite Warehouses
D-6 Custom House
D-7 Louisburg Square
D-8 10 ½ Beacon Street

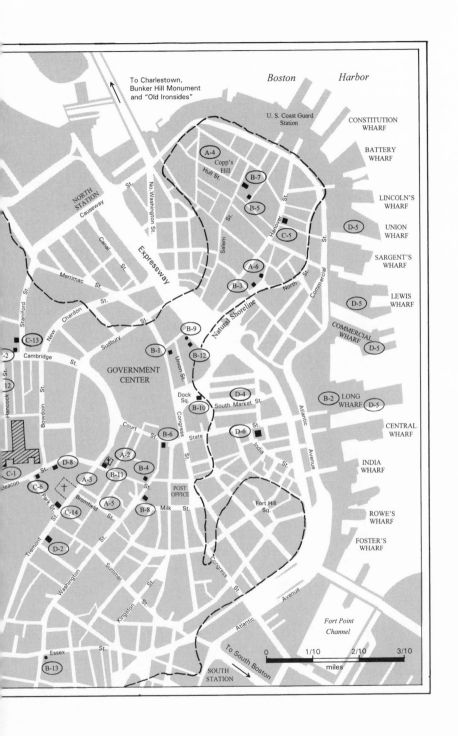

Introduction

By the early 1960s, many aspects of old Boston that I had remembered since early childhood suddenly were threatened by "urban renewal." Auto expressways and the wrecking ball were relentlessly wiping out sections of that wheel-like pattern of streets, lanes, and alleys long known as the Old Hub where important seventeenth-, eighteenth-, and nineteenth-century landmarks still accented the downtown scene. Surely these would be preserved, but many of their nineteenth-century backgrounds soon would be replaced by high-reaching cubes of steel, glass, and concrete, inevitably creating spectacular new skylines and spreading long shadows over the old peninsula and beyond its shores. Not since the great landfills of the early 1800s would Boston see such massive change.

Few tears would be shed over the loss of some blighted areas, yet the prospect of losing certain comfortable nineteenth-century settings—forever—was disconcerting to many and prompted me to begin sketches at once of the most vulnerable sites. Drawings of less-threatened subjects followed, eventually including samples from the Colonial, Provincial, Federal, and Greek Revival Periods, the time spans covered by this work.

Although most of the narrative material that follows is confined to historic landmarks still standing in or near the Old Hub, the material introducing each of the four parts of the book is written more broadly. Thus I have included the wider outside influences of trading, politics, industry, transportation, and changing world fashions during New England's first two centuries of growth.

In compiling a map of downtown Boston streets, I chose to use information reflecting the late 1930s simply because at that time the basic street patterns had been fairly stable for half a century and would remain so until massive obliteration began. Another map—this one covering Boston Harbor, its shores, and its outlying towns—also seemed desirable. It shows several landmarks and communities that, although they lay beyond the confines of the Old Hub, were nonetheless vital to its development and deeply involved in its early

xix

history. On this map one may locate Medford, Somerville, Cambridge, Charlestown, East Boston, Castle Island, Dorchester heights, Brookline, Roxbury, Milton, Quincy, Braintree, Weymouth, Hull, and Boston Light. All are mentioned in the narratives.

Boston's and New England's early leaders relished their roles in shaping their towns' and America's history. Many sat for their portraits, and an astonishing number of these paintings survive in museum collections in or near Boston. This is fortunate because looking a portrait in the eye may often tell us more about a sitter than many pages of words. So wherever such portrayals are pertinent to the written material that follows, their whereabouts, if known to me, will be noted.

The most frequently mentioned sources of information will be abbreviated as follows: MFA, for Museum of Fine Arts, Boston; AAS, for American Antiquarian Society; and MHS, for the Massachusetts Historical Society.

Buildings and Landmarks of Old Boston presents background stories about certain historic landmarks extant in Boston and nearby towns, landmarks that reflect the lives of those early New England leaders—largely Bostonians—who were privileged to influence the course of local and national history from 1630 to 1850. The narratives will focus upon two intertwined themes: the steady movement toward independence, and the more than two-century scramble of Yankee shipbuilders, shipowners, and merchants for a share of the lucrative foreign trade.

Today, in Boston and neighboring ports, handsome mansions still affirm the maritime accomplishments of these acquisitive men and the skills of the capable home designers who served them.

Colonial

(1630–1691)

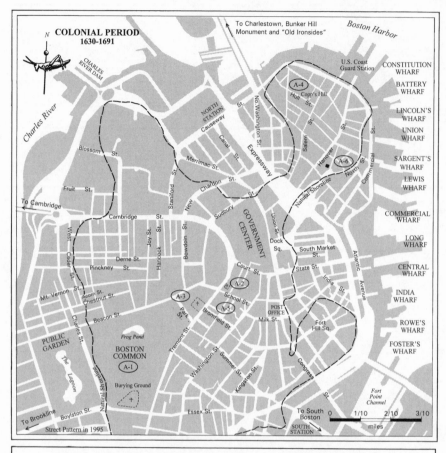

N **COLONIAL PERIOD**
   1630-1691

CHARLES
RIVER DAM

To Charlestown, Bunker Hill
Monument and "Old Ironsides"

Boston Harbor

Charles River

U.S. Coast
Guard Station

CONSTITUTION
WHARF

BATTERY
WHARF

A-4
Copp's Hill
Hull   St.

LINCOLN'S
WHARF

UNION
WHARF

NORTH
STATION
Causeway

Salem St.

SARGENT'S
WHARF

Blossom   St.

Merrimac St.

Canal St.

Chardon St.

Hanover
A-6

LEWIS
WHARF

Fruit   St.

Stanford
New

Sudbury

Natural Shoreline

Commercial

North

COMMERCIAL
WHARF

To Cambridge

Cambridge   St.

GOVERNMENT
CENTER

Union St.

Dock
Sq.

South Market
St.

Atlantic   Avenue

LONG
WHARF

Joy St.

Hancock   St.

Bowdoin   St.

Derne St.

Court St.

CENTRAL
WHARF

West   Cedar   St.

Pinckney   St.

State St.

India   St.

INDIA
WHARF

Mt. Vernon   St.

Acorn St.

Chestnut St.

Park   St.

School St.

A-2

A-3

Bromfield St.

A-5

POST
OFFICE
Milk St.

Fort
Hill Sq.

ROWE'S
WHARF

Beacon St.

Charles St.

PUBLIC
GARDEN

The   Lagoon

Natural Shoreline

Frog Pond

BOSTON
COMMON

A-1

Tremont St.

Washington St.

Summer St.

Kingston St.

Congress

St.

FOSTER'S
WHARF

*Fort
Point
Channel*

Burying Ground

To Brookline

Boylston St.

Essex   St.

To South
Boston

SOUTH
STATION

0   1/10   2/10   3/10

miles

Street Pattern in 1995

A-1 Boston Common   A-2 King's Chapel Burial Ground   A-3 Old Granary Burial Ground
A-4 Copp's Hill   A-5 Province Steps and Gateway   A-6 Paul Revere House

Home of the Cod

N ear the end of the fifteenth century, fishermen in growing
numbers were pursuing Europe's tasty North Atlantic cod,
a fish that was easily preserved in casks of brine and traded
over the sea-lanes of the world.

In early August 1497, when Venetian navigator and trader Giovani
Caboto (John Cabot) returned to Bristol, England, aboard the *Ma-
thew,* following his westward voyage to a North American shore—
perhaps Newfoundland[1]—he reported waters "so swarming with
fish" that they could be scooped from the sea with baskets. Cabot's
exploration had been subsidized by Henry VII, whose primary goal
had been the discovery of a westward sea route to India.

CODFISH FLAKES, AS VISUALIZED BY THE AUTHOR.

In late March 1602, near the end of Queen Elizabeth's reign, English explorer Bartholomew Gosnold, leading a group of thirty-two men, sailed westward from Dartmouth, England, in a small bark, the *Concord*. In mid-May, they dropped anchor near a rocky section of the New England coast where eight friendly Indians, one wearing European clothing, sailed out from shore in a Spanish shallop to greet them. Next day, the *Concord* continued along the coast to a "Mightie headland" of white sand where Gosnold, too, was "pestered" with fish; consequently he called his landing place Cape Cod. One of the nearby islands Gosnold named Martha's Vineyard for his daughter, and there he found a tangle of grapevines, wild strawberries, game birds, deer, a variety of offshore fish, shellfish, and other tasty native foods. Along one north-facing shore that he explored, he found a collection of whale bones. Gosnold named a nearby group of islands after Queen Elizabeth, and traded trinkets with the Indians for furs, cedar logs, and about a ton of sassafras roots, then believed to have great healing qualities. At Cuttyhunk the party built a small fort.

After about a month, however, as vital supplies dwindled, the adventurers set sail for England, where the *Concord* docked at Exmouth "without one cake of bread nor any drink but a little vinegar."[2]

As news of this voyage spread, the spirit of adventure quickened throughout western Europe. Many fishermen were soon drawn to American waters.

Twelve years after Gosnold, Capt. John Smith—soldier, explorer, and a leader in the Jamestown colony—made an able survey of the American northeast coast. Two years later, in London, he published several thousand copies of *A Description of New England,* which included many prints of his famous 1614 map. To encourage fishermen, Smith wrote with canny foresight: "Let not the meanness of the word fish distaste you, for it will afford as good gold as the mines of Potassie."[3] In reporting his own catch of sixty thousand offshore fish in one month, which netted him fifteen hundred pounds, he wrote: "If a man worke but three days in seven hee may get more than hee can spend unless hee will be excessive." He called Massachusetts Bay his first choice above all others for the planting of a colony, and he urged fishermen to establish permanent bases on New England shores, using wintertime for shipbuilding and fur trading with the Indians. Smith also told of one occasion when a French trading ship barely preceded him at the bay and had made off with all the furs! Early traders usually brought the Indians trinkets, guns, rum, and disease.[4]

Some historians believe that seasonal visitations by European fishermen probably had included trading with the natives since 1500, and that about two thousand adventurous fishermen and traders had temporary bases around the shore of the bay when John Winthrop's great migration arrived. At first, such fishing and trading bases barely managed to cling to the shore with the wilderness reaching down to their back doors. Later, with the arrival of their courageous wives and sweethearts who so patiently oriented the drying racks to catch a maximum of sun, many of such bases became lasting colonies.

Because early overland travel between the scattered coastal settlements was accomplished on foot over narrow Indian trails, across fords, and only rarely on horseback, the need for communication by sea was vital. The early settlers were lucky to be well supplied with the natural resources most needed for shipbuilding; fast-flowing streams floated logs to the mills and powered saws to shape the heavy timbers, planks, and masts. New England–built vessels were seaworthy and competitive; soon they would be sought by many of the world's merchants. Codfishing, too, became a major industry in the northern colonies, where each summer the Atlantic shores were white with drying cod laid on racks of loosely woven alders called "flakes." Indeed, colonial fishermen were held in high esteem. During the provincial era in Boston, it was patriotic to eat fish every Saturday. During their busy season, fishermen were exempt from service in the militia. Moreover, their new boats and equipment were free from public taxes for ten years.

By the 1660s, New England merchants were trading cod, lumber, horses, and other farm products in the West Indies for sugar and molasses to make rum. Codfish and rum were then traded in other American colonies, or were shipped to the Gold Coast of Africa where they were swapped for ivory, clothing, spices, gold, and slaves to work on the West Indian sugar plantations. Parliament called this triangular trade "smuggling" since it circumvented British laws designed to force the American colonies to trade only through English ports, where the mother country could exercise more control and collect taxes. Still, the colonists continued to smuggle and, as their fleets expanded, they amassed great fortunes. The British, no doubt holding their noses, called these men the "codfish aristocracy." Actually, though, the Americans had been causing British shippers great alarm. At last, English merchants persuaded King James II to consolidate the northeastern colonies into the "Dominion of New England." In 1686, with the landing in Boston of Sir Edmund Andros as the dominion's governor, all self-government ground to a jolting halt.

Soon after Boston Harbor was blockaded by the British during the Revolution, codfishing dwindled, and when peace at last returned, fishermen seemed unable to regain their old momentum; the world simply had developed other food pleasures. Even so, as a part of the peace agreement of 1783, negotiators John Adams, Henry Laurens, John Jay, and Benjamin Franklin insisted that America's fishing rights off Newfoundland be restored. Adams argued, "We have a saying in Boston, that when the blossoms fall, the Haddock begins to crawl" (to Newfoundland during the hot season).[5] (Benjamin West's portrait of the American negotiators hangs at the Winterthur Museum.)

In the Massachusetts house of Representatives hangs the *Sacred Cod,* a wood sculpture carved by John Welch. When Republicans are in power it points south; when Democrats are in the saddle it points north. This cod has long been an emblem of Yankee initiative for it recalls the olden days when traders would "trye every port." It was made in the mid-1700s to replace an earlier one that had hung at the Old State House before the fire of 1747.

During President Washington's triumphal tour of the States in October 1789, he wrote of joining a group of codfish anglers off Kittery, Maine, "but it not being the proper time of tide we only caught two."[6]

By the 1970s, cod populations in fishing grounds off Newfoundland, Nova Scotia, and Cape Cod were greatly depleted by over-fishing. No longer were cod scooped from the sea with baskets; huge trawling nets were used instead. Despite regulations on mesh size, many small fry were taken up with the rest. These were thrown back, but too many died before they reached the water. Even worse was the failure of fishermen and governments everywhere to effect and enforce broad conservation measures.

The Puritan Venture

Under a grant from King James I to Sir Ferdinando Georges, a mixed company of adventurers led by Sir Ferdinando's son, Robert, sailed westward from England in the summer of 1623 aiming to plant a colony on New England shores. In September, they landed at the abandoned settlement of Wessaguset, now Weymouth, and decided to winter there. But in the spring, when expected supplies failed to arrive, Georges and others sailed back to England. Some, however, chose to remain and establish a permanent colony. Among these, it is thought, was the Reverand William Blackstone, who soon moved northeast to settle on a nearly treeless peninsula

TRIMOUNTAIN AS IT MAY HAVE APPEARED FROM THE CHARLESTOWN SHORE.

known to the Indians as Shawmut, "the place of living fountains." The settlers called it Trimountain, because of its three prominent hills near the mouth of the Charles. Rev. Blackstone was a Cambridge graduate who had brought from England about two hundred books, various tools, seeds, and other supplies needed for a quiet, independent life.

In mid-June 1630, about a decade after the Pilgrims first stepped ashore at Plymouth, Gov. John Winthrop,[7] leading several waves of Puritans in 11 ships, also reached Massachusetts shores. Winthrop wrote that his fleet carried about 700 persons, 240 cows, and 60 horses. This migration had been authorized by Charles I and among its most prized possessions was the company's 1629 charter bearing the seal of the king. Today, this famous document is affectionately preserved in the Archives Museum at the New State House, Boston.

Winthrop's following included well-to-do families, skilled artisans,[8] and indentured servants willing to work their way to eventual independence. Most were members of the English middle class, and 75 percent were literate. Some sought religious freedom, others sought a better lifestyle than the current economic climate in England could offer, and still others sought land.[9] The fondest wish of some Puritans, however, was religious conversion of the Indians.

Governor Winthrop's ship, the *Arbella,* was the first to anchor off Naumkeg, now Salem. But much sickness was found there so the company sailed southward to Charlestown,[10] earlier known as Mishawan, and there the Puritans began to build their shelters. When a dearth of fresh water developed, scouting parties were sent out to explore the countryside. A small boat crossed the mouth of the Charles River where a young girl leaped ashore to become the first Puritan to set foot on the Shawmut peninsula. Many years later Ann Pollard recalled her first impressions of that terrain: "Very uneven, abounding in small hollows and swamps with blueberries and other bushes." A portrait of Ann, painted when she was 103, is preserved at the MFA.

By 1630, Blackstone was well settled at Trimountain, where he enjoyed ample supplies of fresh water, a cottage, and his flourishing farm; his orchard still bore fruit in 1765. Upon learning of the

Puritans' need for water, he invited them to settle near him. Some, including Winthrop, quickly accepted. Others chose to remain at Charlestown or move to Dorchester, Roxbury, Cambridge, Watertown, Medford, or Saugus. Still others returned to England.

At a meeting of the Court of Assistants held in Charlestown on September 7, 1630, the name Trimountain was changed to Boston.[11]

Two years later, Boston had become the seat of government for all the surrounding settlements and a fort was being built on an isolated rise about eighty feet above the harbor. Today, although the rise is gone, the site is still called Fort Hill.

As time passed, Blackstone regretted his welcome of the Puritans. His quiet, hermitlike existence was threatened by Puritan rules and religious activities. In 1634, for thirty pounds, he sold them his rights to all the lands on the peninsula except six acres on Beacon Hill that included his cottage. He then bought cattle and moved south to settle near what is now Providence.

Roger Williams recorded Blackstone's death at age eighty in Cumberland, Rhode Island, on May 26, 1675. One and a half centuries later, when Mill Creek in Boston was landfilled, it was renamed Blackstone Street.

The Massachusetts Bay Colonies

When the first Puritans arrived at Trimountain, they found little wood for fuel or housing. Each spring, Indian farmers had burned off the woodland undergrowth to encourage tender new shoots as a lure for deer and other wild game. Choice meadowlands, reserved for growing squash, beans, and corn, were also burned off regularly at planting time. Limited stands of timber were found on the harbor islands, but soon it was necessary to forage farther inland using simple river barges as carriers. At least Blackstone had led them to the Great Spring, where water was abundant and sweet. A path that led there is still called Spring Lane.

Historians have uncovered no drawings showing just what the first rude shelters of the Puritans were like. We do know that some settlers brought tents and others may have adopted Indian designs using indigenous building materials. The natives simply covered

A CONJECTURAL
VIEW OF THE EARLY
BOSTON SETTLEMENT.

bell-shaped or arbor-shaped frames of green saplings inside and out with water-repellent mats of tightly woven reeds. Some practical colonists are thought to have dug their wood-buttressed homes into the south-facing slopes of hills. Thus little more than one facade of mats was exposed to the elements.

When more sophisticated homes could be built, hand-hewn frames were covered with boards inside and out. Between the studs, a wattle of split saplings often was constructed to hold a daub of clay and chopped marsh grasses for better insulation. Roofs were thatched with coarse grasses and reeds gathered along the shores of swamps and tidal estuaries. Simple one-room houses of that time were usually warmed by a fireplace opening into a boarded end-chimney lined with clay. If additional wood could be afforded, floors, too, were planked against the cold and dampness. Windows, often glazed with oiled paper, were few and small. During the long winter nights, such homes were likely to have been lighted by bayberry candles or torches made from dried rush stalks dipped in fat. At bedtime older children simply climbed a ladder to their sleeping quarters in the loft. Crude household furnishings, usually cut from pine, were starkly functional at best.

Despite the efforts of chimney inspectors, fires were frequent and catastrophic. Laws forbidding thatched roofs were passed but they were not enforceable; many settlers just could not afford better houses. Eventually stone or brick chimneys rising from cedar or slate roofs became the rule. With the advent of waterpower, refined homes were quite possible for well-to-do colonists. For example, the 1640 Whipple House on Ipswich Green almost could have been plucked from medieval England, and a scattering of such houses may still be found in New England seaboard towns. Ipswich claims 110 houses built before 1790, and 55 of these were completed before 1720. Many of the still-surviving early New England houses are wood-framed "saltboxes" faced with narrow clapboards and oriented if possible, to give the southern facades a maximum of winter sun, while their long north roofs slope down to within a few feet of the ground. In the beginning, the saltbox had a one-room, end-chimney plan. Then, as a family outgrew its living space, a second section was built beyond the chimney. Later, a lean-to was added to the back facade to bring the kitchen and woodshed under one roof. The practice of designing a second-floor overhang on some front facades suggests a carry-over from Elizabethan times in England, when space between the houses was vital for coach travel on very narrow streets. For added protection and warmth, the main access door was double boarded, using vertical boards outside and horizontal ones inside.

As time passed, chimneys became more complicated: multiple flues carried smoke from several ample fireplaces on two floors. The interior walls of these houses were often plastered with a mixture of clay and goat's hair, then finished with a whitewash of ground clamshells and water. Natural light entered through small windows made of tiny diamond-shaped or rectangular-shaped panes of glass set in leaded casements; roof dormers, being wasteful of heat, were seldom used by thrifty New Englanders. Fieldstone cellars, however, were vital for retaining ground warmth and for preserving vegetables and fruits.

As the Puritans' first winter progressed, Boston women endured a bleaker life than they had ever known: bitter cold, poor housing, scarcity of food, sickness, and high mortality tested them severely.

Throughout the early colonial time, New England women were relatively few; spinsters were rare indeed. Most women lived a strenuous and often short life, yet more women continued to arrive. They raised and clothed large families; tended farm animals; helped with the harvest; dried fruits; made breads, pickles, and candles; then spent their evenings spinning, weaving, and sewing. Widowers were encouraged to remarry and bachelors even became objects of discrimination. In Hartford, "lone men" were taxed twenty shillings per week, and in 1695 the village of Eastham, Massachusetts, voted that single men must kill six blackbirds or three crows each year.

English laws of that time were designed to force colonists to buy expensive cloth woven in the mother country. However, because most Americans could not afford such luxury, woolen and linen homespuns became a necessity. Flax for linen cloth could be home-grown successfully on small garden plots, and most family members were expected to take some part in the many steps needed to produce the finished material.

English class distinctions were still strong in the early years of some colonies. People without substantial assets were not permitted to assume the more elegant dress styles of the upper classes, which included such influential people as merchants, shipowners, lawyers, and members of the clergy. Even so, social mobility upward was more rapid in America; wealth and property could be accumulated in less than a generation, and they often were. Historians now believe that only about one in five of those who colonized the wild shores of Massachusetts Bay did so in search of religious freedom. The rest, they think, differed little from the pioneering doers and achievers who, in all eras, have sought more gainful employment and a better life elsewhere.

When the Puritans first settled at Trimountain, no natives were seen. Later, small tribes weakened by European diseases were found farther inland. These Indians were friendly and eager to trade dried corn for tools, tinkling bells, and other trinkets. This exchange was fortunate, for without native corn many more Puritans would have succumbed to their first severe winter in Boston.

The Puritans steadily expanded their settlements: clearing forests to establish farms; damming streams for mills; and building bridges and stone boundary walls.[12] Such was their understanding of God's will. Of course, all great human migrations have been accomplished at the expense of the tenants they displaced. In Massachusetts, the Indians were expected to adopt Christianity and to be industrious servants as well. But the natives, seeing their territories being occupied, eventually grasped the full meaning of the European incursions. Hostile raids on frontier settlements began; the Puritans retaliated with superior firepower, and thereafter relations with the "savages" were most un-Christian. French Catholic missionaries were often more successful, for they approached the Indians as equals, living among them to win them as friends and allies for the long struggle against the English and the Americans.

Boston Common

In the southwest quadrant of the Old Hub lies the ancient Common. At one time, this included all of Old Granary Burial Ground, Tremont Street, Park Street, and some of Beacon Hill. By 1737, Sentry Street—now Park Street—separated Old Granary from all the rest, but since that time no other street has been allowed to divide this nearly fifty acres of public land.

After the Puritans bought first settler Blackstone's land rights in 1634, their leaders laid out space for a training field, a cow pasture, and a public meeting place where Puritan lawbreakers might be whipped or locked into stocks or pillories for all to see. In the 1660s, a visiting English botanist, John Josselyn, wrote about young Boston swains who walked their sweethearts here at sunset, "[t]ill the nine o'clock bell rings them home to their respective habitations, when presently the constables walk their rounds to see good orders kept, and take up loose people." Other early visitors to Boston described the terrain as almost treeless; Ann Pollard suggested a pasturelike aspect. Bonner's 1722 map shows only three trees on the Common, the largest being the Great Elm[13] standing near the powder house. But a mid-nineteenth-century engraving, executed not long after the cows had departed, shows many young trees developing on the open slope below the Frog Pond. Except for major early-nineteenth-century excavations on the summits of Beacon Hill and Mount Vernon, the natural contours of Blackstone's pasture are probably less changed today than any other original features of the Hub.

Since its beginning, the Common—or Green—has mirrored a long series of actions and events that helped to shape the town and the nation. When word reached Boston that the French fortress at Louisburg, Cape Breton Island, had fallen to the English and the New Englanders on June 16, 1745, a huge bonfire was lighted on the

BOSTON COMMON, NORTHWARD VIEW FROM FROG POND.

Common. Bell ringing, parades, music, fireworks, and refreshments added to the fun.

In 1756, the triangular-shaped Central Burial Ground, adjacent to Boylston Street, was begun on the Common. About twenty years later, many British soldiers of the Revolution were interred here in a common grave. Rhode Island–born Gilbert Stuart, the painter, also lies here in an unmarked spot.

In 1758, after the second capture of Louisburg Fortress from the French, Gen. Jeffrey Amherst sailed into the port of Boston with his great fleet of warships and transports; his forty-five hundred men pitched their tents on the Common before their march to Albany.

In mid-May, 1766 when John Hancock's brig, *Harrison,* arrived in Boston with news that the Stamp Act had been repealed in Parliament, great rejoicing filled the town. Flags flew, bells rang, cannon roared, candles were lit in windows around the Green, the Sons of Liberty displayed Paul Revere's candle-lighted paper obelisk, wine flowed from the Hancock cellar, and fireworks surpassed all such spectacles within memory.[14]

On October 1, 1768, following Boston riots and frictions over parliamentary duties and taxes, an armed fleet of eight British ships arrived from Halifax with troops and artillery. These soldiers, finding no welcome in private Boston homes, raised their tents on the Common or were quartered in public buildings and empty warehouses.

When General Gage closed the harbor in 1774, the Common again became a campground for the king's troops. Of this time Dr. Oliver Wendell Holmes later wrote:

> And over all the open Green,
> Where grazed of late the harmless kine,
> The cannon's deepening ruts are seen,
> The warhorse stamps, the bayonets shine.[15]

On the night of April 18, 1775, British soldiers embarked from "the open Green" to cross the Charles and begin their march on Lexington and Concord. Only a little earlier, rebels had stolen two cannon from the British arsenal on Boston Common. These were smuggled out of town in a load of manure and named Hancock and Adams. Today, these cannon stand in the room atop Bunker Hill Monument.

After France became America's ally in 1778, Admiral d'Estang and his fleet sailed into Boston Harbor for repairs and supplies. The French were thought to survive on frogs and salads, so Bostonians were pleasantly surprised to welcome such handsome and vigorous sailors. But, true to tradition, the men were soon discovered searching the shore of the Frog Pond.

Mrs. John Hancock was asked, on rather short notice, to entertain three hundred officers of the fleet for breakfast at her home on Beacon

Hill. Lacking enough milk, she sent servants to the Common to milk all the neighbors' cows. (Copley's portrait of Dorothy Quincy Hancock now hangs at the MFA.) Admiral d'Estang then asked leading Bostonians to be his guests for dinner on shipboard. Afterward Abigail Adams wrote, "We went according to invitation and were sumptuously entertained."16

In the 1830s, the ancient privilege of pasturing cows on the Common was ended. Certain ladies had complained that the cows "misbehaved."

In late October 1848, when water from the Cochichuate Reservoir was first piped into town, a valve was opened at the Frog Pond. A column of water and spray surged eighty feet into the sky and a waterworks historian later described the scene: "After a moment of silence, shouts rent the air; the bells began to ring; cannon fired; and rockets streamed across the sky."17 A handsome hand-tinted lithograph of this spectacle, hanging at Old City Hall, shows clusters of men wearing tall beaver hats; women wearing bonnets, capes, and shawls; columns of soldiers in bright uniforms with black fur headgear, and thousands of citizens watching in awe. Apparently there was a grand display of fireworks in the evening. Public buildings and many private homes were lit brilliantly. Soon the comforts of indoor plumbing were a fact of life on Park Street.

Today, the Common still offers rest and recreation for young and old, pedestrians still find it a convenient shortcut to Back Bay, and in summer snoozers and lovers still dream on grassy slopes between the walks.

King's Chapel Burial Ground

Boston's oldest burial ground, lying just north of King's Chapel on Tremont Street, was begun in the fall of 1630 when young Sir Isaac Johnson is said to have been buried here in land he had set aside for his garden. Also buried here are Governor Winthrop and later governors; prominent clergy; Lady Andros; John Alden of Plymouth; Mary Chilton, the first Pilgrim to set foot on Plymouth

KING'S CHAPEL
BURIAL GROUND.

Rock; patriot William Dawes; and many other worthy colonists. Tradition has it that even Captain Kidd, the pirate, is buried here. As the cemetery began to fill, there was a saying going around, which went along the lines of, "Brother Johnson's garden is getting to be a poor place for vegetables."

In 1877, the board of health proposed that this and other old Boston burial grounds be taken for public use, "for sooner or later the remains of those buried in these cemeteries will be removed and the ground used for other purposes."

In the late 1970s, in a similar vein of thought, the ancient marble and sandstone tombstones marking the site of Governor Winthrop's remains were demolished by cemetery workers and replaced with modern stones of heavy granite.

The Shillings, the Diary,
and the Witches

John Hull, a successful shipowner, merchant, and distinguished Bostonian of the mid-1600s, is probably best remembered as the "mintmaster."

In 1652, as coins became scarce in the colony, Hull and his partner, Robert Sanderson, were directed by the general court to design and mint Willow, Oak, and Pinetree shillings—also called Bay shillings—plus other coins of lesser value.[18] Later, as the operation expanded, the court required a wood-framed mint house to be built east of Kingston Street on land that Hull had purchased in 1653.[19] It was to measure sixteen feet square by ten feet high.

These coins, being illegal, were disturbing to King Charles II until he was soothed by Sir Thomas Temple, an agent for the general court, who told him that the design symbolized the royal oak. Hull's coins were minted from a bullion of various monies and their purity compared favorably with British issues of the same denominations. Their sterling standard weights, however, were about one quarter less than the English coins. Moreover, they were costly to produce. The mintmaster was paid about fifteen pence for every shilling minted and tradition says his plump daughter's dowry was paid in Pinetree shillings equal to her weight.[20] In any case, it is certain that young Samuel Sewall became Hannah Hull's husband.

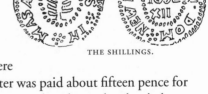

THE SHILLINGS.

Years later Sewall wrote in a letter to his son, Samuel Jr., about the memorable day at Harvard years before when Hannah had seen him receive his degree, although he didn't know she had "set her affection" on him until they were married on February 18, 1675/6.

In the summer of 1661, when he was nine years old, Seward and other members of his family had sailed from England aboard the *Prudent Mary*. When at last they were met in Boston by Samuel's father, Henry, they were taken to the ancestral farm in Newbury, where Henry had preceded them by about two years. Samuel's grandfather had established the farm in 1634.

At about age twenty-two, Samuel Sewall began his now famous fifty-six year journal, which includes his daily activities and important happenings in Boston and nearby towns. Because Sewall was a successful merchant and held important public offices, his diary is especially interesting to historians. He knew the foreign traders of Boston and the cargoes of their fleets; he was intimate with Indian educator John Eliot, the Mathers, and other influential clergymen of his day; he recorded important news from abroad, the decimating epidemics of smallpox, and the advent of paralyzing blizzards that blanketed the town; he provided insights into seventeenth-century lifestyles; he described the bloody incursions of Indians upon frontier settlements; and he reported the demise of King Philip, the great Wampanoag Indian chief. On May 1, 1697, he received former Indian captive, Hannah Dustin, who, aided by Mary Neff and a young boy, recently had axed to death ten Indians and brought back their scalps. (Before the end of the seventeenth century, hostile actions from Indian tribes in New England had been effectively and brutally eliminated.)

An interesting period in Sewall's writings was the interval of six years between 1686 and 1692. The colony had lost its charter in 1684 following serious friction with England over colonial rights—a loss whose impact became even more clear with the arrival in Boston of the British frigate *Kingfisher* in late December 1686. Stepping ashore was the newly appointed governor of the Dominion of New England, Sir Edmund Andros, whose arbitrary ways soon would provoke further animosity in the town. In mid-April 1689, after learning that James II of England had fled his throne, Bostonians locked up their governor for nine months before shipping him back to England

THE 1629 MASSACHUSETTS BAY COMPANY CHARTER.

aboard the *Mehitable*.[21] But those abrupt actions were not recorded in Sewall's daily journal because, in late November 1688, he had sailed to England aboard the *America* to attend to family matters and to offer his assistance to Increase Mather and others in their efforts to obtain a new colonial charter.[22]

While Sewall sailed eastward, James II fled to France, soon to be succeeded by his daughter, Mary, and her husband, Prince William of Orange. On the day before the successors were proclaimed Queen and King, Sewall wrote of seeing Princess Mary pass by on the Thames in her barge, "Ancients and streamers flying, bells ringing, guns roaring."

THE 1642 SALEM WITCH HOUSE.

During the Salem witch trials of 1692, when nineteen people were condemned to death by hanging, Sewall was one of the judges. Five years later, he confessed his terrible mistake in a statement read to the congregation at South Church by Rev. Samuel Willard—the same pastor who would baptize Benjamin Franklin only hours after his birth.

Hannah and Samuel Sewall found much enjoyment in farming and other rural pursuits as they gradually acquired extensive property in outlying towns. In 1687, they bought a major part of Hog Island, now Breed's Island, and planted chestnuts there. Five years later Sewall bought about five acres of Beacon Hill land, calling it Elm Pasture. In 1711, the Sewalls sold some of their pasture to the town to enlarge Copp's Hill Burial Ground. A part of this land, is still called Hull Street, after Hannah's father, John Hull.

Sewell wrote the first antislavery pamphlet ever published in America, *The Selling of Joseph* (1700). Toward the end of his life, he served ten years as chief justice of the Superior Court of Judicature.[23] When John Hull and Samuel Sewall died, they were buried in Old Granary on Tremont Street.

Old Granary Burial Ground

Old Granary Burial Ground on Tremont Street, first known as Old South Burial Ground, was started in 1660. Early settlers, Revolutionary War patriots, statesmen, and forebears of many people who walk the streets of Boston today are buried here. Among the more celebrated are Paul Revere, John Hancock, Samuel

OLD GRANARY
BURIAL GROUND

Adams, John Hull, Samuel Sewall, John Smibert, Peter Faneuil, James Otis, Robert Treat Paine, Crispus Attucks (lying in a common grave with his four companion victims of the Boston Massacre), and Benjamin Franklin's mother and father.

Somewhat over a century ago, a row of English elms growing along Tremont Street by Old Granary were still shading this historic ground. Earlier, they had shaded the hay market, then the wood market. Later, they cooled people waiting to board the horse cars. Known as the Paddock Elms, they had been imported from England around 1762 by Adino Paddock, a prominent coach builder and captain of the Artillery. From his nearby shop on the opposite side of Tremont Street, Adino kept a sharp watch over his young saplings. Sometimes he would hurry from his door and vigorously shake little boys who molested them. Some say that descendants of those elms are still shading parts of Old Granary and the Common.[24]

In the olden days, all Boston cemeteries were rented out to farmers for pasturage and haying. In the nineteenth century, perhaps to facilitate haying operations, many headstones were moved to obtain more uniform rows. Today, this famous landmark is a playground for squirrels, a nesting place for birds, and a quiet spot to be enjoyed from the windows of the Athenaeum, the Park Street Church, and the nearby office buildings.

Copp's Hill

opp's Hill, known originally as Mill Hill and then as Snow Hill, is the northernmost promontory of the Boston peninsula that overlooks the Charles river estuary, Charlestown, and Bunker Hill.

At Copp's Hill in 1634, Boston's first windmill ground corn for the colonists. By the mid-1640s, one could look westward from here to Mill Pond, where early settlers used a causeway dam with tidal gates to power their mills. Waters passing through those mills flowed across the peninsula through Mill Creek to the harbor. As late as 1794, three mills were still operating at Mill Pond. One made chocolate.

COPP'S HILL BURIAL GROUND.

The burial ground on Copp's Hill originated in 1661 and was first known as Old North Burial Ground. Eventually Copp's Hill— as the cemetery came to be known—became the largest of the early cemeteries.

Among the many noteworthy persons buried here are Increase Mather[25] and his son, Cotton. Both were austere and strict Puritan clergymen and both were prolific writers; Cotton published 388 works. In April 1688, the Massachusetts Bay Colony sent Increase to England aboard the *President* to protest the administration of Governor Andros, and to plead for a renewal of the original 1629 charter. His efforts were rewarded in some degree by the granting of the 1691 Province of Massachusetts Bay Charter, which greatly increased the Puritans' territory. Although his writings on witchcraft fostered a widespread delusion that led inevitably to the Salem executions, Cotton Mather deserves much credit for the growth of culture and education in New England. In 1721, Cotton persuaded 286 Bostonians to receive inoculations against smallpox; this test possibly hastened worldwide acceptance of the treatment.[26] During their lifetimes, the Mathers were probably the most powerful manipulators of religious thinking, education, and politics in all of New England.

Weather vane maker Shem Drowne, too, lies at Copp's Hill, as does Robert Newman. On the evening of April 18, 1775, Newman climbed the steep stairs to the belfry of Christ Church where he hung two lanterns for Paul Revere, and looked over this quiet, moonlit ground.

Another buried here is Daniel Malcom, a successful merchant and a Son of Liberty. In 1768, he advocated a ban on importing British goods. He also led troublemakers at Liberty Riot, when customs officials seized John Hancock's sloop *Liberty* for smuggling Madeira wine in 1766. Tradition says the scars on Malcom's headstone were inflicted by British bullets. Still another interred here is Edmund Hartt, the builder of Old Ironsides, and yet another is George Worthylake, in 1716 the first keeper of Boston Light.

On the harbor side of Copp's Hill lies Charter Street, where for many years stood the mansion of Sir William Phips, a man of varied talents. Born in the Maine woods and afforded almost no formal education, he nevertheless was endowed generously with self-confidence and native intelligence. After trying carpentry, coastal trading, and shipbuilding, and feeling in no way intimidated by his limited credentials, Phips sailed to London in the mid-1680s seeking backing from Charles II and the admiralty for his scheme to salvage sunken treasure from the Spanish galleon *Conception,* wrecked in 1641 on a coral reef about eighty miles north of Hispaniola (now the Dominican Republic and Haiti).

The British indeed were persuaded and King Charles loaned Phips the frigate *Rose.* But the expedition failed and returned to England. Meanwhile Charles had died, so with little pause Phips sought help from James II for further exploration of the site. In 1687, Captain Phips sailed westward for another try, this time aboard the *James and Mary,* and this time with astonishing success. Three hundred thousand pounds worth of Spanish gold, silver, and gems was raised from the forty-six-year-old hulk and Phips was awarded twenty thousand pounds as his share. Moreover, he was knighted by James II at Windsor Castle. Before long, Sir William returned to Boston to build his wife a brick house on Green Lane, now Charter Street.[27]

In May 1690, Sir William, serving William and Mary, led a successful expedition to capture Port Royal in Nova Scotia; but his August attack on Quebec was a dismal failure. Later, in England, King William commissioned Sir William to be the first royal governor of a new province that included Plymouth Colony, Massachusetts Bay Colony, Maine, and Nova Scotia.

In early March 1692, accompanied by Increase Mather and convoyed by the frigate *Nonsuch,* Sir William sailed back to Boston to assume his high office under the new charter.[28] Before long, when his wife was suspected of being a witch, he simply abolished the witch trials. Within about two years, Phips became unpopular and was recalled to England where he died suddenly in 1695. Later, his widow married Peter Sargent, the wealthy Boston merchant whose 1679 mansion eventually became Province House.

When the French and Indian Wars at last drew to a close, word reached Boston that Quebec had fallen to the English on September 18, 1759. To celebrate, a huge bonfire was lit on Copp's Hill. Two cords of wood, fifty pounds of gunpowder, and forty-five tar barrels insured its success. Thirty gallons of rum and great quantities of beer were also consumed and the province paid for all!

From Copp's Hill, on the morning of June 17, 1775, General Burgoyne looked down to North Battery as three regiments of British regulars and a battalion of marines prepared to embark for the fight at Breed's Hill. Of that scene Oliver Wendell Holmes later wrote:

> At eleven the streets were swarming, for
> the red-coats' ranks were forming;
> At noon in marching order they were
> moving to the piers;
> How the bayonets gleamed and glistened,
> as we looked far down and listened
> To the trampling and the drum-beat of
> the belted grenadiers! [29]

By early afternoon, Burgoyne's cannon had bombarded Charlestown with firebombs, while Admiral Graves's six men-of-war had fired red-hot balls to hasten its destruction. [30]

Later, the remains of Charlestown were sketched by Lieutenant Williams of the Royal Welch Fusiliers from the British redoubt on top of Beacon Hill. He showed a desolate forest of chimneys at the foot of Breed's Hill, but little else.

From the summit of Copp's Hill in the 1780s, Bostonians proudly watched the building of the great Charlestown toll bridge. When it was officially opened on Bunker Hill Day, 1786, this wooden span had a thirty-foot draw and was admired by engineers everywhere. To celebrate, thirteen salutes were fired from Breed's Hill; thirteen others then answered from Copp's Hill; bells rang from both towns; and a great parade marched from the Old State House to the Bunker Hill Monument, where a feast was spread for nearly eight hundred people accompanied by Boston youngsters chanting, "You Charlestown Pigs put on your wigs and come over to Boston Town." After dark the bridge was lighted by "40 elegant lamps." In time, moreover, the bridge proved to be a financial success.

In January 1793, an ox was roasted on Copp's Hill to celebrate the success of the French Revolution. The horns were then raised over Liberty Square on a sixty-foot pole.

Province Steps and Gateway

The ancient stone steps and iron rails at Province and Bosworth Streets are thought to be the only remains of an upper passageway leading to the estate of Peter Sargent, a well-to-do seventeenth-century merchant and later a judge at the Salem witch trials. His palatial three-story house, built of Holland-molded bricks

PROVINCE STEPS
AND GATEWAY.

INDIAN ARCHER WEATHERVANE,
AGAINST ITS POSSIBLE BACKGROUND.

in 1679, stood on land which at one time was owned by Governor Winthrop. It faced the corner where Old South Meeting House now stands. A more elaborate wrought-iron gateway adorned the front approach. Thus we find that only forty-nine years after the founding of Boston, great wealth was being realized from foreign trade; shipowners and merchants were building the forerunners of early Georgian-style houses to flaunt their success. Elegant interior paneling, furniture, china, and silverware, as well as portraits by John Smibert, were commonplace in these homes.

About two years after Sargent's death in 1714, the property was acquired by the Province of Massachusetts. Soon it became known as Province House, where royal governors, important visitors, and British generals had their headquarters. Here, on cold winter evenings, liveried servants passed spiced hot rum, French and Spanish wines, and champagne among guests seated around the blazing hearth.

From 1716 to 1845, Shem Drowne's famous Indian archer weather vane stood above the cupola and aimed its arrow toward the winds. The four-foot, gilded-bronze figure with drawn bow and quiver has amber-colored eyes and is preserved at the MHS. "A gilded Indian . . . with his bow and arrow on a string, as if aiming at the weather cock on the spire of Old South." (Nathaniel Hawthorne, *Twice Told Tales.*)

For many years, the royal arms hung over the front entrance to Province House and there it remained until news came that independence had been declared. On that riotous day it was barely saved from vandals. Today, it is preserved at the MHS.

Paul Revere House

P aul Revere's early home in North Square was built by John Jeff about 1681 or earlier. It is Boston's oldest wood-framed house. Revere acquired it around 1770 and lived here about thirty years. Most of his children were born here.

Until the great fire of November 27, 1676, clergyman Increase Mather, too, had lived on this site. Despite a heavy rainstorm, Mather's house and about fifty others in the North End were lost that day.[31]

Within the walls of the ancient but well-preserved house, furnished in simple colonial style, are numerous small items and several important pieces said to have been owned by the family.

Paul Revere, son of Apollos Rivoire,[32] a French immigrant, was born in Boston in 1735. Except for a short assignment in the infantry as a second lieutenant at Crown Point during the French and Indian Wars in 1756, Paul remained in Boston to help carry on the family's goldsmithing business following his father's death in 1754. He became a capable goldsmith, an engraver, a denture maker, and a bell founder. His foundry stood at Lynn and Foster Streets where nearly four hundred bells were cast by Paul and his son, Joseph Warren Revere.[33] Many of these bells still resound from New England steeples.[34] Revere was also a Son of Liberty, a confidant of statesmen, a secret courier, and a molder of colonial thinking in favor of independence.

In early September 1774, the rebellious and forceful Suffolk Resolves, proposed by patriot leader Dr. Joseph Warren and aimed against coercive British acts, had been adopted by a provisional congress held in Milton. These resolutions were promptly carried by veteran express rider Revere to the First Continental Congress at Carpenter's Hall in Philadelphia, where they quickly were endorsed by the delegates on September 17. Thus delegate John Adams could

PAUL REVERE HOUSE.

write in his diary, "This was one of the happiest days of my life."[35] By that time, the steeples, taverns, bridges, and milestones along the Boston Post Road were familiar landmarks to Revere.[36]

On the morning of April 16, 1775, he rode to Lexington carrying secret information to Hancock, Adams, and others about British plans to raid military stores in Concord on April 19. Thus quantities of armaments were hidden or carried from the town by local militia before the redcoats arrived three days later. On his way home, Revere stopped briefly in Charlestown to complete arrangements with other patriots for flashing lantern signals from Christ Church in Boston. His next sally to Lexington would be made famous by Longfellow's poem "Paul Revere's Ride."

In his later years, Revere prospered from his copper mills in Canton, where he also enjoyed country living. At age eighty, during the War of 1812, he helped plan harbor defenses for Boston.

Three handsome portraits of Revere hang at the MFA: Copley's canvas of the young craftsman holding a silver teapot, St. Memin's chalk profile, and Gilbert Stuart's superb 1813 oil showing Mr. Revere in his late seventies. A portrait of Revere's second wife, Rachel Walker Revere, also hangs at the MFA.

The Provincial Powder House

In 1703, John Mallet began to raise his stone windmill on Quarry Hill in Charlestown, now a part of Somerville. When completed, this slate-slab structure had three oaken floors supported by heavy oaken timbers. It was eventually deeded to the Province of Massachusetts to be used as a public storehouse for gunpowder.

PROVINCIAL
POWDER HOUSE.

On August 31, 1774, after learning from Tory informer William Brattle[37] that Charlestown, Medford, and other nearby towns gradually had been withdrawing their private powder supplies from this storehouse since July, British general Thomas Gage suddenly ordered 260 soldiers to embark from Long Wharf before dawn. They were to row 13 boats up the Mystic River, then march westward over Winter Hill to seize the 250 half barrels of powder that remained. Actually, this was only the king's share, but as false rumors of horrible Boston killings spread, about 4,000 militiamen from all over New England—carrying muskets, pitchforks, and clubs—crowded the highways for a march to Cambridge. There, in their fury, they surrounded the home of Lieut. Gov. Thomas Oliver and by threats of violence compelled him to sign a written resignation from the governor's council. Today, Oliver's portrait hangs at the MFA and his mansion still stands in Cambridge on Old Tory Row.

The powder house scare was short-lived, but rebel leaders and the people of Boston were much encouraged by the spirit of unity that the outpouring had displayed. Moreover, the patriots were immediately spurred into action on other fronts. In a matter of days, for example, Joseph Warren's nineteen powerful Suffolk Resolves were sped by Revere to the Congress in Philadelphia, and the training of minutemen was quickened throughout the towns and villages of the province.

On November 18, 1774, George III told his prime minister that New England was in a state of rebellion, and "blows must decide whether they are to be subject to this country or independent."[38]

Provincial

(1691–1783)

PROVINCIAL PERIOD
1691-1783

To Charlestown, Bunker Hill Monument and "Old Ironsides"

Boston Harbor

Charles River

To Cambridge

To Brookline

To South Boston

U.S. Coast Guard Station

CONSTITUTION WHARF
BATTERY WHARF
LINCOLN'S WHARF
UNION WHARF
SARGENT'S WHARF
LEWIS WHARF
COMMERCIAL WHARF
LONG WHARF
CENTRAL WHARF
INDIA WHARF
ROWE'S WHARF
FOSTER'S WHARF

Fort Point Channel

0   1/10   2/10   3/10
miles

Street Pattern in 1995

SOUTH STATION

B-1 Capen House   B-2 Long Wharf   B-3 Moses Pierce-Hichborn House   B-4 Old Corner Book Store
B-5 Clough House   B-6 Old State House   B-7 Christ Church   B-8 Old South Meeting House
B-9 Boston Stone   B-10 Faneuil Hall   B-11 King's Chapel   B-12 Ebenezer Hancock House
B-13 Liberty Tree

The Provincial Era

After the independent-minded Massachusetts Bay Colony had lost its charter in 1684 because of intransigent behavior toward the Crown, and until the arrival of Sir Edmund Andros as governor of the Dominion of New England in 1686, an interim government over the colony headed by Pres. Joseph Dudley, a native of Roxbury, was decreed by King James. Andros's tenure as governor lasted less than two and a half years, so again, briefly, the

SHIRLEY-EUSTIS HOUSE.

colony was on its own. Then, largely due to the nearly three and a half years of delicate negotiations in London between colonial agent and clergyman Increase Mather and King James, and later with that monarch's successors, William and Mary, a new charter for a provincial government over most of New England was at last signed in 1691. Thus, the provincial era began in Massachusetts, where a total of eleven royal governors would be empowered to serve the Crown before Gov. Thomas Gage resigned in October 1775. (The first of these was the fabulous Sir William Phips, a native of Maine.) All were harassed by the uncooperative legislatures and courts of the province.

On September 25, 1690, about a year and a half before Phips left England to take up his duties as governor, the first newspaper ever published in America was printed in Boston by Richard Pierce—its title, *Public Occurrences Both Foreign and Domestick*. Although only one issue was ever printed and only one copy is known to have survived, Pierce expected to publish his newspaper once a month or more often if a "glut of occurrences" demanded it. But the general court disapproved of its content, so that was its demise. On April 17, 1704, Bartholomew Green of Boston became the editor and publisher of the first permanent weekly newspaper in America. This was the *Boston Newsletter*, "Published by Authority." Green's office then stood on what is now Washington Street at Avon Street. In 1721, the weekly *New England Courant* was first published by James Franklin on Queen Street, now Court Street. James's brother, Benjamin, was apprenticed there at age twelve, and there, too, Benjamin's anonymous contributions under the name of Silence Dogood were published in 1722.

In the summer of 1696, the court ordered that a market be held in Boston on Tuesday, Thursday, and Saturday mornings, and that this be opened by the ringing of a bell. Local farm people and fishermen offered turkeys, mutton, lamb, beef, veal, offshore fish, shellfish, cheeses, and occasionally bear meat. In the summertime, melons, apples, cherries, pears, peaches, grapes, and other fruits were displayed as well.

In the early 1700s, as the colony prospered, simple colonial-style farmhouses were more spacious and convenient than the familiar saltbox designs. Many had two full floors of living space and some had attics.

Strangers visiting Boston during this first quarter of the eighteenth century were impressed by its expanding shipyards and rope walks, its spreading waterfront docks, and its great volume of foreign and domestic trade. In fact, by the 1730s, its thirteen thousand people had made it the most populous town in America.[1]

By mid-century, however, England's unruly province had greatly increased its competition with London merchants and traders throughout Europe, Africa, and West Indies. At last, with pressure from the influential British Board of Trade, which regulated commerce at home and abroad, England strengthened its restrictive laws to counter the increasing provincial thrust. To a noticeable extent these rules were successful, but not before numerous New England shipowners and merchants had acquired huge trading fleets and substantial wealth, much of which they spent to build one or more mansions in Boston or in the surrounding countryside.

Meanwhile, as England's war with France worsened, American traders simply ignored the trade laws with relative impunity.

As classical revival trends strengthened, impressive houses took on a more ornate look. Instead of the colonial central chimney plan, two or more chimneys might emerge from a four-sided hipped roof, leaving a middle section surrounded by an ornamental balustrade to conceal buckets of sand and water for fighting fires. Important interior rooms might be graced with carved cornices, wainscoting, and inlaid floors. Sophisticated clocks, cabinetwork, silver, and rare chinaware were imported from England, and family portraits by Copley were avidly sought. Also, in keeping with all the rest, there were lovely private gardens, servants, and beautiful horses and carriages. In summary, what eventually became America's century-long fascination with embellished Georgian-style homes was inspired by the wealth of its prosperous men who made such attributes a hallmark of their success.

Among the few examples of such mid-eighteenth-century clapboard-sided homes still standing in or near Boston, perhaps the most celebrated is the Shirley-Eustis House on Shirley Street in the Roxbury section (see illustration on page 41).

In 1731, William Shirley arrived from England to begin what proved to be a successful law practice in Boston. He was appointed to be the seventh royal governor of the Province of Massachusetts Bay a decade later, and in 1746 work on Shirley Place, his Roxbury country seat, was begun.

From the windows of this handsome Georgian mansion, possibly designed by Shirley's friend, Peter Harrison, the governor and his family could look out on their 330-acre estate terraced with gardens and enlivened by a 250-foot, spring-fed canal crossed by bridges, or they could look northward over Roxbury Flats to the church steeples and the three hills of Boston. With his glass, Shirley might spy the cupola of Province House, his official downtown residence. (A gilded-iron banneret vane that at an earlier time turned over Shirley Place, may be seen at the MFA.)

William Shirley was one of the more popular royal governors. In 1745, he promoted a successful forty-two-hundred-man expedition to capture Louisburg Fortress from the French and later, following the death of General Braddock, he was briefly a major-general in command of all military operations in the colonies.

Since 1819, when Shirley Place was sold to Governor William Eustis, it has been known as the Shirley-Eustis House. It still dominates its Roxbury knoll about fifty feet above sea level. Down through the centuries, despite a long procession of tenants and fashion changes, the basic structure of this house was somehow preserved until the 1980s, when extensive restoration work was at last pressed forward.

Three years after George III inherited the throne in 1760, the Treaty of Paris gave all of Canada to the English. As a result, New Englanders could fish off the Grand Banks to their hearts' content, and King George would forever be a popular monarch in Boston, or so it seemed. Not until James Otis inflamed Bostonians against the Writs of Assistance did provincials begin to feel that their basic rights as Englishmen were menaced. The lives of provincial women, however, were constantly threatened by uncertainties and dread: those living along the frontiers faced the hazards of Indian warfare, and later, as the French and Indian Wars ended, women of Boston were swept into those troubled times that led to the Revolution. As the differences between rebel and loyalist thinking became more evident, some shopkeepers and merchants leaned toward the British point of view; yet their wives and daughters were reluctant to take a stand that could mean the loss of their homes. Moreover, the courage of all women in Boston would soon be tested severely. Hard on the heels of General Gage's redcoats fleeing Concord and Lexington came minutemen and militia eager to throw a siege ring around the peninsula. A mutual exchange of loyalist and rebel families was then arranged by General Gage. Although many of those transfers were successful, it was apparent that numerous rebel-oriented households would be held as hostages to avert firebombing threats.

During the eleven months that the British held Boston, both rebel and loyalist townspeople were subjected to constant indignities, robberies, and insults. They suffered, too, from extreme cold, serious shortages of food and fuel, and a takeover of their public buildings and some churches for military use. North Meeting House and the ancient home of Governor Winthrop were taken down for fuel, and only one school remained in operation. According to a ballad of the time,

> And what have you got, by all your
> designing,
> But a town, without dinner, to sit down and
> dine in?

Bostonians were not really forgotten, however: in the winter of 1774, the people of Marblehead sent 207 quintals of codfish to help relieve the shortages.

Capen House

The red-brick Capen House on Union Street dates from the early 1700s. Among early enterprises conducted here was an importer's store offering fine clothing and silks.

In the 1770s, in this building, Isaiah Thomas published *Royal Magazine* and an anti-British underground newspaper called *The Massachusetts Spy*. In the latter paper, he was a relentless and uncompromising champion of local patriots who pressed for colonial rights and independence. Being a close friend of Paul Revere, Thomas often printed that patriot's inflammatory engravings in his newspapers. By mid-April 1775, sensing the real dangers in his secret work, Thomas suddenly packed his press and fled to Worcester, where he continued to publish his views in safety. In later life, Thomas prospered; by 1800 he had produced nearly a thousand books and was destined to become the largest American publisher of his time. His old wooden press and his 1780 office building are now preserved at the Old Sturbridge Village Museum.[2]

Another who lived briefly at Capen House around 1800 was a young exiled French duke who, with his two brothers, was on a tour of America. While awaiting expected funds from home, he taught French at this house.

The duke's two-thousand-mile journey took him westward to the Mississippi and included a visit with George Washington at Mount Vernon. While there, notations in his diary reveal shock at the lot of slaves in southern states. (In 1786, George Washington wrote that he kept 216 slaves on his plantation.) The duke also observed that Americans never walked if they could ride.

After returning to France, the duke was appointed lieutenant general by Charles X, but that monarch was overthrown by the July Revolution of 1830. Before long, with support from Lafayette, the duke

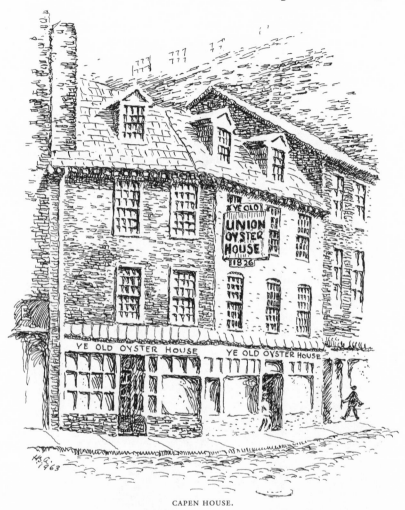

CAPEN HOUSE.

was chosen "Louis-Philippe, king of the French."[3] Philippe eventually became unpopular. In 1848, he abdicated. He has the distinction of being the last king of France.

Since 1826, a restaurant at Capen House has offered oysters and other seafoods to delight Boston's most critical tastes. (In earlier times oystermen peddled their day's catch from door to door out of shoulder packs.)

Long Wharf

Long Wharf, first known as Boston Pier, stands at the foot of State Street on Boston's waterfront. Construction was begun in 1710, and a part of its basic fill is rubble salvaged from the great fire of 1711.

As foreign trade expanded, Long Wharf also grew. Only a decade after it was started, it had been extended eight hundred feet, and by mid-century it had reached eighteen hundred feet eastward into the harbor.

The deepest hulls could berth there at any stage of tide, and by that time the number of vessels sailing annually from the port of Boston had grown to over a thousand.

Along the north side of Long Wharf stood shops, counting

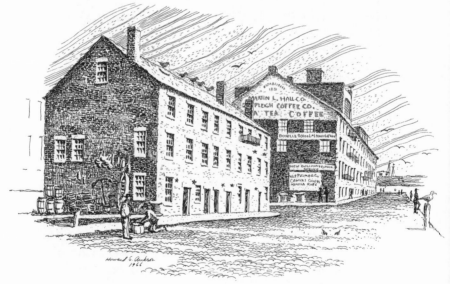

LONG WHARF.

rooms, and warehouses. All were serviced by an always busy thirty-foot roadway that in the evening became a public promenade. Foreign dignitaries and important guests from other colonies, disembarking here, were escorted directly up King Street, now State Street, to the Town House to present their credentials.

On October 1, 1768, as the rebellious spirit of Boston's people mounted, Colonel Dalrymple and two regiments of British troops with cannon landed at the wharf from Halifax and marched through the streets with fixed bayonets. This was the event so vividly portrayed by Paul Revere in his famous engraving,[4] still widely reproduced by print dealers and publishers.

In describing those tense days, lawyer John Adams wrote that every morning he was awakened by a British drum and fife in front of his house in Brattle Square, and in the evening he was serenaded by the violins, flutes, and songs of the Sons of Liberty under his windows.[5]

In mid-May 1774, General Thomas Gage arrived at Long Wharf aboard HMS *Lively* to replace Governor Thomas Hutchinson. Thus Gage became the eleventh and last provincial governor.[6] On June 1, he blockaded Boston Harbor and declared Salem to be the new capital of the Province of Massachusetts Bay. On September 1, he ordered British soldiers to embark from Long Wharf to seize the king's supply of gunpowder at Charlestown's Quarry Hill storehouse and convey it to Castle William in Boston Harbor. Another part of Gage's forces was transported from here on June 17, 1775, to fight at Breed's Hill; and on March 17, 1776, Washington watched Gen. William Howe evacuate his occupation troops and numerous loyalists from this pier.

Following the Revolution and the rebuilding of New England's fleets, Long Wharf merchants again sought commerce in foreign ports, especially in the China trade, where great fortunes were reaped by a few Boston families. In the 1830s and 1840s, shipowner Ezra Weston, also known as King Caesar, kept counting rooms and warehouses here.

The Chart House, currently a restaurant, is a recently restored red-brick building on Long Wharf. This structure, probably built late in the eighteenth century, is considered to be the oldest brick warehouse on the waterfront.

Around 1975, a 30"× 50" landscape painting of the Boston skyline and Long Wharf, probably observed from Noddle's Island in the late 1730s, turned up in Washington, D.C., where it was offered for sale on behalf of a New Orleans art dealer. Art experts and historians currently call it the first known American landscape painting and attribute it to John Smibert. Long Wharf with its warehouses, Christ Church, and other landmarks of the time can easily be identified in this harbor scene. In 1995, this painting was housed at the MFA.

Another early rendering of Long Wharf and the steeples of Boston was the excellent 1743 print produced by William Price and offered at his print and map shop near Old State House. In this view we find Fort Hill, Old South, the original King's Chapel, Old State House, Beacon Hill with its beacon, Hancock House, Christ Church, and a lively harbor filled with sail.

Moses Pierce–Hichborn House

Little is known about the early occupants of this house built in 1711 by Moses Pierce, a glazier. His mother was a daughter of John Jeffs, who earlier owned the land and also built the Paul Revere house next door. Hichborn, a boatbuilder, was a cousin of Revere.

In 1949, Hichborn descendants began a restoration of the house, which may be viewed by the public at certain times. It has a huge eighteenth-century kitchen fireplace, a simple Jacobean staircase, plain plastered walls, and, in some rooms, beveled wood paneling. Simple interior furniture of the period may also be seen in this modest but well-built red-brick home.

MOSES PIERCE–HICHBORN HOUSE.

Old Corner Bookstore

Standing at the foot of School Street is the original Old Corner Bookstore building. In 1637 on this site stood the home of William Hutchinson and his wife, Anne, who became a disruptive religious leader in Boston by advocating the importance of God's grace, which was a direct challenge to prevailing religious beliefs. After long discord, Governor Winthrop and the Puritans banished her to Rhode Island in 1638.[7]

OLD CORNER BOOKSTORE.

Anne's lineal descendant, Thomas Hutchinson, was the unpopular tenth royal governor of the Province of Massachusetts Bay, who was recalled to England in 1774.

Just before the great fire of 1711, Thomas Crease, an apothecary, owned a wood-framed house on this land.[8] When that building was lost in the blaze, Dr. Crease, as he was known, began the present red-brick one. Although the date of its completion is unknown, several later owners continued to dispense drugs here some years before other enterprises took over.

In 1828, a bookstore and a printing shop were opened here by Carter and Hendee, thus introducing a period of bookselling and publishing that continued under various owners until 1903. Outstanding among them in mid-century were the partners William Ticknor and James Fields. The latter was a catalyst who brought successful writers together. As editor and publisher, he was fair with authors and this trait brought him the finest writers of America and England. Legend says much credit for his success was due to his wife, Annie Adams Fields, an accomplished writer and a charming hostess to her husband's literary friends. The *North American Review* and the *Atlantic Monthly* were also published here.

Old Corner attracted great numbers of book lovers. In return, they gave it many prosperous years.

By the mid-1950s, the building was nearly hidden behind massive signs hung on the School Street and Washington Street facades, and decay had brought talk of demolition. Alarmed preservationists united in 1960 for a fundraising drive, and the building was restored a few years later. Currently it houses a branch newspaper office and a small museum.

Clough House

Edward Clough, a stonemason, lived for a time in this three-story red-brick house. It was one of six identical houses that he built in back of Christ Church for speculation. All the others are now gone. Clough was a Son of Liberty, a member of the Tea Party, and an expert builder who helped lay bricks for Christ Church. Benjamin Franklin owned a house next door to Clough House for a while, but that property was taken down when Revere Mall was created in 1933. Clough House was restored by fund-raising in 1971.

CLOUGH
HOUSE.

Old State House

At the head of King Street, now State Street, Puritans of the 1630s who disobeyed the rules of the Brethren were often publicly whipped or locked into stocks or pillories and ridiculed by the townspeople.

In the spring of 1635, the general court ordered that an outdoor market be held here each Thursday.

As time passed, this marketplace became central to all of the town's business. About 1654, following a great fire in Boston, when Robert Keane, a tailor and commander of the Artillery, began planning his

THREE VIEWS (PAGES 55-57) OF THE OLD STATE HOUSE.

Howard S anders
1963

Howard S. Auden
1963

will, he left money to help the town build a water conduit leading from the top of Cotton Hill to a wooden reservoir (for fighting fires) located in the marketplace, and he left funds for a wood-framed townhouse, which was built there in 1657. John Hull, the mintmaster, was one of five men appointed to oversee its construction. An open-air market occupied the ground floor and above that, supported by twenty-one massive wood columns, was the meeting place of the general court and the Artillery. But the Town House, as it was called, was destroyed in the great fire of 1711 and plans for a red-brick one were soon begun. The designer is unknown but overseer William Payne is known to have been given a major role in its construction. On May 5 of the following spring, Samuel Sewall wrote, "I lay a stone at the southeast corner of the Town House and had engraven on it S.S. 1712." By December 6, the outer walls were apparently well along. On that day Sewall wrote, "Mr. Holyoke observes the eclipse in the Town House turret." Then, on May 5, 1713, Sewall's journal suggests that the new building is nearly finished: "Dr. Cotton Mather makes excellent Dedication-Prayer in New Court-Chamber." Again, on May 29, he wrote, "Dr. Increase Mather prays Excellently in the Council."

On February 6, 1714, Sewall and others gathered here on the Queen's birthday to drink to her health. Before long, the Town House must have fairly hummed with activity. Just under the roof were rooms useful as extra space for town business; on the second floor, provincial courts were held in a room on the west end where a quiet view of the Cotton Hill pasture could be enjoyed; the royal governor and his council gathered at the east end overlooking the busy merchant fleet at Long Wharf and the island-dotted outer harbor where other sail awaited their turn to berth. The general assembly met in the large middle room, as did the selectmen when the assembly was not in session. On the first floor, merchants gathered at one o'clock to buy, sell, and exchange goods, or simply to learn the latest news from abroad. In the cellar, a wine shop offered relaxation from all the rest.9

The Town House was seriously gutted by fire in 1747, but restoration began at once and today its walls date largely from 1713.

Here, before Chief Justice Hutchinson and other members of the court in February 1761, James Otis, Jr., delivered his impassioned four-hour address against the British Writs of Assistance, which allowed customs officials to search private properties for evidence of tax evasion on imported goods. John Adams was present in the council chamber that day, and years later he wrote of judges in scarlet robes and massive wigs sitting around a great fire while full-length portraits of Charles II and James II seemed to gaze down from "Splendid gold frames" upon those historic deliberations. "Otis was a flame of fire! . . . American independence was then and there born."[10]

From the east balcony on July 18, 1776, at exactly 1 p.m., Col. Thomas Crafts first read the Declaration of Independence to a large gathering of Bostonians as cannon roared from harbor ships, batteries, and forts.[11] Among the many invited guests that day were several captured British transport officers on parole, who reported that people were excited, beaming, and dressed in their "holiday suits." Soon after the ceremony, the people of Boston tore the royal lion and unicorn from the east end and burned them in the street. On July 4, 1776, King George III had written in his diary that nothing important happened that day."

In the autumn of 1789, while on a grand tour of the States, President Washington arrived at Old State House astride his white charger, accompanied by the French Fleet band.[12] Great throngs filled the streets to see their president, but the official reception was less than flattering. State and town officials squabbled over the marching order, thus causing a serious delay in starting the long parade. As a result, Washington, Vice President Adams, and patriot Samuel Adams were caught in a cold, drenching rain. Then, Governor Hancock dawdled over making a courtesy call. But when it became clear that the president would wait in lofty dignity to receive him, Hancock finally relented, so the story goes, and blamed his tardiness on the gout.[13]

In 1793, the state and the town agreed to a swap: Old State House and Province House were given to the town in exchange for a new state house site on Beacon Hill. However under town ownership Old State began a steady decline. For years it was used by shopkeepers, whose signs were hung or pasted on its outer walls.

In 1830, the city council voted to ask architect Isaiah Rogers to remodel it in classical revival style for a town hall. However, the city government needed the building for only ten years, so Old State resumed its slow decay. By the early 1880s, it had reached such poor condition that even demolition was considered. Second thoughts developed, though, when Chicagoans offered to buy and move it to Illinois!

By 1882, a major restoration was underway, including a return of the lion and unicorn to the east end—but not without the addition of a gilded American eagle over the west entrance.

Today, this beloved landmark houses a fine museum, an excellent research library, and the Bostonian Society, an outgrowth of the dedicated group who fought for preservation in 1881 and 1882.

Christ Church or Old North Church

Christ Church (also known as Old North Church), is an ancient landmark on Salem Street near Copp's Hill. It is generally thought to have been designed by William Price, a vendor of maps and prints of early Boston.

Construction was begun in 1723 and now it is the oldest church left in the Hub. Bricks for its massive thirty-inch-thick walls were hand-molded at a Medford yard and its huge interior timbers were hewn from Maine pine. Nearly twenty years were required to complete the main structure. Last of all came its far-reaching spire, long a welcome beacon for fishermen and merchantmen sailing into port.

When the steeple was blown down by a hurricane in 1804, Charles Bulfinch designed another; a 1954 hurricane took down that one, too. Today's replacement is taller, stronger, and closer to the original proportions than the Bulfinch design. A Shem Drowne weather vane still spins high above the street, and in the cellar, we are told, burial vaults still hold about eleven hundred bodies, including many British who fell in the Revolution.

On April 18, 1775, when it became clear to rebel leader Joseph Warren that the redcoats were preparing to row over the Charles and march on military stores in Lexington and Concord, he dispatched two fast couriers to spread the alarm. William Dawes galloped to Lexington by way of Roxbury and Arlington while Paul Revere rowed over the Charles to reach Lexington through Charlestown and Medford. In addition, Revere had directed sexton Robert Newman to flash lantern signals from the steeple of this church to other patriots on the Charlestown shore:

OLD NORTH CHURCH (CHRIST CHURCH).

By the trembling ladder, steep and tall,
To the highest window in the wall,
Where he paused to listen and look down
A moment on the roofs of the town,
And the moonlight flowing over all.
(H. W. Longfellow, "Paul Revere's Ride")

Legend says that as Revere prepared a boat for his moonlit crossing, he felt the need to muffle his oars while passing downstream from the sixty-four-gun HMS *Somerset* anchored in mid-current. Help was requested; a flannel petticoat, still warm, was thrown from a window, and Revere's crossing continued undisturbed.

In Lexington, Revere and Dawes were joined by Samuel Prescott for the remainder of the journey, but only Prescott would alert Concord that night: Revere was arrested by British scouts. After being questioned for several hours, he was released unharmed but deprived of his horse. Dawes escaped but was forced to retreat to Lexington.[14]

Old South Meeting House

Old South Meeting House, known as Old South, stands at Washington and Milk Streets on land where Governor Winthrop had tended his garden. (His residence was taken down by British soldiers for firewood in the severe winter of 1775.)

Being the third and southernmost of the Boston churches, it was known as Third or South Church. The original church was built of cedar in 1669. In a small house on the opposite corner at Milk Street, a son was born to Josiah and Abiah Franklin on January 17, 1706. He was baptized that wintry day by Rev. Samuel Willard. The baby was named Benjamin.[15] South Church was dearly loved by the congregation, but by 1728 committee members reluctantly voted forty-one to twenty to take it down because of serious decay.[16]

The current building, designed by Robert Twelve, was built in 1729. A Shem Drowne banneret vane still whirls above its steeple.

In the mid-1700s, Rev. Thomas Prince kept a study and a public library in the steeple. His books and documents, which he called the New England Library, proved invaluable to scholars. Thomas Hutchinson used them while researching his *History of the Colony of Massachusetts Bay.* Among rare manuscripts that Prince preserved was Gov. William Bradford's *Of Plymouth Plantation,* so very useful to many historians.[17]

Shortly before the Revolution, this priceless record disappeared and was lost until 1844 when it was located in the private library of the Bishop of London. A copy in longhand was at last obtained by the MHS in 1856, and in 1891 the original, too, was returned to Boston.

On many occasions Old South played a vital role in crystallizing colonial sentiment for independence, for only here could patriot orators rally and shelter really large masses of people for the causes of liberty.

OLD SOUTH MEETING HOUSE.

In mid-June 1768, James Otis, Jr., addressed a large gathering at this site, assailing Parliament's heavy-handed enforcement of the Writs of Assistance and the impressment of Boston men aboard the *Romney*, a fifty-gun British warship.

GOVERNOR HUTCHINSON'S
CARRIAGE HOUSE (SUPPOSEDLY).

In the afternoon of March 6, 1770—the day after the Boston Massacre—a huge crowd of furious citizens organized by Samuel Adams met at Old South, demanding removal of the redcoats to Castle William in the harbor. This was soon done.[18]

After 1600, when the East India Company was chartered by Queen Elizabeth, tea drinking enjoyed a steady rise in England and the colonies. By the early winter of 1773, however, the London warehouses of the company fairly bulged with an enormous glut of tea! The government then decided that this could be unloaded readily in the colonies at a reduced price, at the same time generating a tax at each port of entry. But Parliament seemed unaware of the growing gap between British and American sentiments.

Although a British-inspired law forbade shipowner Rotch's *Dartmouth* to leave the dock before its tea was put ashore, the patriots summoned Rotch before them on December 14 demanding that he apply at customs for permission to clear the harbor with his cargo. Customs officials refused. About ten o'clock on the morning of the sixteenth—as a last resort—the patriots directed Rotch to journey to Governor Hutchinson's country seat on Milton Hill high above the Neponset River estuary. There Rotch begged the governor's understanding, but Hutchinson, too, was inflexible.[19] Meanwhile, by mid-afternoon, about seven thousand townspeople had congregated in or near Old South to listen to the rousing speeches of their leaders. Around six o'clock, when Rotch as last returned to the meeting to report his failure, Samuel Adams rose, saying, "This meeting can do nothing more to save the country."[20] About fifty men in Mohawk paint then whooped from the building and raced to Griffin's Wharf. There, with others, they boarded Rotch's brigs, *Dartmouth* and *Beaver,* and a small vessel, the *Eleanor,* owned by John Rowe. Working quickly, "the Indians" split open 342 chests of East India Company tea and dumped them into the brine.[21]

The next day John Adams wrote, "The die is cast. The people have passed the river and cut away the bridge."[22] On that same day, Paul Revere saddled up to carry the news to New York and Philadelphia. His round-trip took eleven days but he returned with a promise that New York, too, would refuse the tea.[23]

When Governor Hutchinson's official report on the Tea Party reached England aboard the *Haley* on January 19, 1774, the British were furious. In particular, they vented their rage on Benjamin Franklin, a respected colonial agent in London, who was abruptly dismissed from his duties as deputy postmaster general of North America.

Other responses were slow but sure. In mid-May 1774, the *Lively,* which had sailed from Plymouth, England, at last reached her berth at Long Wharf. Stepping ashore was Thomas Gage, captain general and governor in chief of His Majesty's Province of Massachusetts Bay, sent to replace Governor Hutchinson, who had taken refuge at Castle William. Gage was saluted by shore batteries and harbor ships, then escorted to the Town House by John Hancock's cadets. From there, he was taken to Faneuil Hall where a dinner had been prepared in his honor. After that, changes came rapidly: on June 1, Gage closed the port of Boston, and before the end of summer, he was joined by eleven regiments of British troops.[24]

When these occupation measures were proposed in Parliament, Edward Burke had risen to say that enacting them would forever alienate the colonists from England.

Late one afternoon about seven months after the Tea Party, circuit lawyer John Adams, who had ridden many miles and had at last reached his place of lodging, asked, "Madam, is it lawful for a weary traveller to refresh himself with a dish of tea providing it has been honestly smuggled or paid no duties?"[25] The lady replied, "No, we have renounced all tea in this place, but I'll make you a cup of coffee."[26]

In the early afternoon of March 5, 1775, the fifth anniversary of the Boston Massacre, patriot Joseph Warren climbed through a window at Old South to address a meeting so large that he could not enter by the door. His subject was tyranny. Also present were Selectmen John Hancock and Samuel Adams. Suddenly, with the arrival of a group of British officers, the scene took on the look of an emergency, but Adams politely offered the officers the best seats while Warren's natural acumen and impromptu wit carried the meeting to an orderly close.[27]

During the great Boston fire of 1872, when horse-drawn fire trucks were greatly limited by an equine illness called the epizootic, sixty Boston acres were totally burned. However, with great effort from numerous heroic people, Old South was saved.

A few years later, the congregation voted to sell Old South and rebuild in Back Bay. But even as demolition began in 1876, an aroused public was rallied to fight for preservation of the building. Old South now houses a fine museum.

Boston Stone

The stone ball imbedded in a wall of the red-brick home at 9 Marshall Street was brought from England in 1635, so the story goes, and was used by painters to mill their pigments in a stone trough, a section of which now supports the ball.

In 1692, Thomas Child, a house painter, lived in a house at the corner of Marshall and Union Streets, where he hung his painter's arms—now preserved at the Old State House Museum. Perhaps Child, too, rolled this ancient ball to prepare his paints. He died in 1706.

BOSTON STONE.

Tradition suggests that the location of the stone was at one time very close to the center of town and that it was accepted as a reference point by surveyors of early days. The engraved name and date are thought to have been added later by a local tavern keeper to mimic an even earlier stone at the center of London. For a while the Boston Stone was lost, but it turned up when a foundation for the present house was dug. In 1835, it was placed in its current spot to help protect the building from wagon traffic.

Faneuil Hall

When Faneuil Hall was built in Dock Square in 1742, it was presented to the town by the affluent merchant, Peter Faneuil.[28] As designed by John Smibert, the Scottish artist who painted portraits of over 275 prominent New Englanders,[29] that red-brick hall could shelter 1,000 people. Faneuil tied strings to his gift: a public meeting place was to occupy the second floor and stalls for a market were to be built below. Although severely burned in 1761, the hall was restored two years later with funds raised by a public lottery. Charles Bulfinch strengthened and enlarged it in 1805.

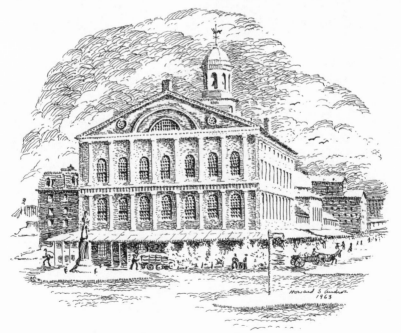

THREE VIEWS (PAGES 71, 72, AND 74) OF FANEUIL HALL.

Here in the 1760s, the patriots repeatedly stirred the people of Boston against oppressive rulings of the Crown. James Otis, Jr., called it the Cradle of Liberty and so it is known today.[30] The third-floor museum is the meeting place of the Ancient and Honorable Artillery Company, which has had headquarters here since 1746. Under a charter granted by Governor Winthrop, this company was organized in the summer of 1638 to protect the colony. Traditionally, on June 1, after attending a church service, the governor and the company marched to the Common to elect officers, who then treated the men to "punch made of old West Indies and new England rum, Havana sugar, and lemons or limes for souring."[31] In later times, this company trained officers for the French and Indian Wars and after that, for the Revolution. The Artillery is the oldest military organization in the United States and it still marches each year in colorful uniforms.

At the west approach to Faneuil Hall stands a svelte bronze version of Samuel Adams, the Grand Incendiary, which little resembles the plain, pudgy manipulator painted by Copley.[32] For a decade before the Revolution, Samuel Adams ceaselessly prodded and agitated the colonies toward believing that independence could and should be seized. He was a prime organizer of the Sons of Liberty, the Boston Tea Party, and the Committees of Correspondence; he served four years as a delegate to the Continental Congress in Philadelphia, and later three times was elected governor of Massachusetts.

In the early winter of 1818, Josiah Quincy and artist John Trumbull drove Samuel's eighty-three-year-old cousin, John Adams, to Faneuil Hall for a special preview of the artist's painting, *The Declaration of Independence,* which had been commissioned by Congress for the rotunda of the Capitol. To complete his canvas, on which Jefferson, Franklin, and John Adams are so prominently portrayed, Jefferson had provided Trumbull with a pen sketch of the room where the signing began. To obtain the likenesses of thirty-three other signers, Trumbull persevered for thirty years.

The gilded grasshopper vane still turning above the cupola was made of copper by artisan Shem Drowne. As a symbol of trade, it resembles another that spins over the Royal Exchange in London.

In the mid-1900s, during a periodic restoration, a metal box was discovered in the belly of the insect; it was labeled "Food for the Grasshopper" and inside were newspapers of the 1880s, coins, and other such items.

Only a few years ago, Bostonians experienced a jolting shock: their beloved grasshopper was missing! Police detectives quickly spread their nets to catch the thief. Days passed. Then a certain steeplejack painter supplied a clue. Shem Drowne's grasshopper was found under some old flags in the cupola and all was well again in the marketplace. (Cambridge, too, boasts of a Shem Drowne vane, a huge 1721 cockerel that crows above the 1870 stone church near the upper end of Cambridge Common. It is thought to have spun much earlier over Christ Church in the North End of Boston.)

King's Chapel

The old granite chapel at the corner of Tremont and School Streets is the second King's Chapel built on the site.

Puritans of seventeenth-century Boston wanted no Anabaptists, Quakers, or other sects to settle on their peninsula. Whenever such people were discovered, they were driven from the town; several were even sent to the gallows and buried under the Common. Not until 1687, when British governor Sir Edmund Andros arbitrarily

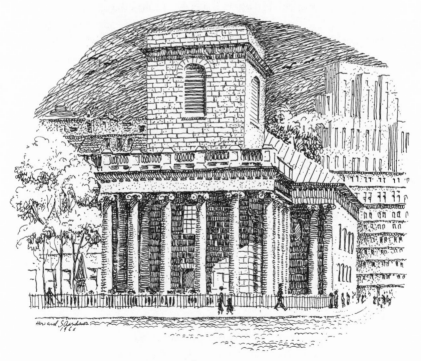

KING'S CHAPEL.

took over space in South Church for his Anglican services, did the Puritans reluctantly give way.

In 1688, Andros usurped a corner of the Puritan's burial ground and ordered a simple wood-framed chapel built there for his parishioners. A cockerel weather vane surmounting the steeple turned above a crown.[33]

In 1710, the chapel was enlarged fifteen feet to the north and ten feet to the east, but by 1741 serious decay in the old building compelled the congregation to consider a new structure. The membership of the church included several wealthy men who pledged generous contributions for raising a new chapel at the old site. The donors included customs collector Sir Henry Frankland;[34] merchant Charles Apthorp; merchant Peter Faneuil, whose family home stood on Tremont Street opposite the chapel site; and William Shirley, seventh royal governor of the Province of Massachusetts Bay.

In 1749, a cornerstone for King's Chapel was at last laid at the northeast corner. That stone, now thought to be buried under eight feet of landfill, was set with much ceremony by the governor, who then invited the workmen to drink his health. Peter Harrison—sea captain, amateur architect, and Shirley's friend—had been engaged to draw up a design for a granite-walled chapel that would have a steeple. But delay followed delay and no funds for the spire were ever raised.

Granite for the four-foot-thick walls came from pasture boulders found in Braintree (now Quincy), where crude methods were devised to fracture the huge stones. According to legend, great fires were built around them; then heavy iron balls were dropped by derrick from above. The fragments were sledded out of the pastures on the winter snows to barges on the shore. This was reputed to be the first granite quarried in this country.

As construction began, a stone shell was raised around the old church, which was then broken to bits and thrown from the windows. Thus few sermons were missed. To accommodate the new chapel, the old Latin school was dismantled too.

During the unpleasant years of British occupation, local people pointedly called King's Chapel "the Stone Chapel."

Forty years after the cornerstone was laid, President Washington attended an oratorio at the chapel, which was held to raise funds for a portico designed by Charles Bulfinch. The president wore a black velvet suit and gave five guineas to the cause.

When the chapel bell was cracked by an eager ringer in 1814 it was recast by Paul Revere and Sons, and on his bill Revere is said to have written, "the sweetest bell we ever made." When Revere died in 1818, this bell was tolled eighty-three times for the years of his life. Its mellow sound may still be heard in Boston.

Although the chapel's congregation has been Unitarian since 1787, numerous reminders of its Episcopalian heritage may still be seen within the ancient granite walls. A scrubbing of the outer walls in 1975 revealed many richly colored stones, perhaps a confirmation of the legend about fire-heated boulders.

Just back of the chapel, Richard Greenough's homely bronze likeness of Benjamin Franklin stands on the site of the first Latin school in Boston where Franklin, as an eight-year-old, studied under Nathaniel Williams. Benjamin not only went to the head of his class; he was soon advanced to the next grade.

Ebenezer Hancock House

The red-brick house at 10 Marshall Street was built by John Hancock in the late 1760s. Previously the site was owned by his uncle, Thomas Hancock, who had willed it to him in 1764. John later transferred title to his brother Ebenezer. At one time, this building served as an inn, where Washington and Lafayette are said to have been frequent guests.

In the late summer of 1778, America's new French ally, Admiral d'Estang, sailed into Boston harbor aboard the ninety-gun flagship *Languedoc,* accompanied by his fleet. He brought cannon for a harbor fortification at Hull and a loan of French silver crowns for a much needed back payment to Washington's Eastern Continental Army. These monies were delivered to Ebenezer Hancock, then deputy army paymaster, and were stored in this house.

Since 1821, a shop has occupied the ground floor continuously. In recent times, a country-style store has operated here.

EBENEZER HANCOCK HOUSE.

Liberty Tree

Liberty Tree and the Sons of Liberty are remembered today by a bas-relief at the corner of Washington and Essex Streets, formerly Hanover Square. Here in the 1760s stood a handsome group of elms. One was named Liberty Tree, the area that it shaded was Liberty Hall, and the men who met there were the Sons of Liberty. Before they were united by John Hancock and Samuel Adams against a common enemy, they had been members of rival gangs from the north and south parts of town. Yet, when presented with a worthy cause, they proved very effective in stirring up trouble over unpopular parliamentary edicts such as the Navigation Acts, the Writs of Assistance,[35] and the hated Quartering Act.

Although the French and Indian Wars had ended with the Treaty of Paris in 1763, colonists along the American frontiers had continued to face Indian tribes so hostile that only strong military establishments could keep the warriors at bay. As a result, in 1764 Parliament levied a sugar tax on the American colonies to help defray the costs. In the following year, a stamp tax was also imposed, but autonomy-minded Americans, especially New Englanders, not only resented revenue stamps, they refused to comply.

As early as December 4, 1754, following a journey to talk with Gov. William Shirley in Boston, Benjamin Franklin wrote to the governor complaining further about parliamentary oppressions imposed on the colonies, about prohibition of trade with foreign markets other than England, and about all taxation without colonial representation in the home government.

In addition, during the decade before the Revolution, dissident New England patriots made excellent use of a willing local press — especially the popular *Boston Gazette,* which published letters from Josiah Quincy, Jr., John Hancock, James Otis, Joseph Warren, Samuel

LIBERTY
1766
LAW ORDER
SONS of LIBERTY 1766
INDEPENDENCE of their COUNTRY
1776
H.S.Andros

LIBERTY TREE.

and John Adams, and other outspoken New Englanders. Their views were then copied by other newspapers and widely read throughout the colonies.

In Parliament, too, in 1766, some members defended the rights of Americans to disobey laws passed by a governing body in which they had no legal vote. William Pitt was one of these.

To honor the Sons of Liberty, and to recognize the ninety-two members of the Massachusetts legislature who, in February 1768, refused to withdraw their resolutions to import no taxable British goods, fifteen Sons of Liberty commissioned Paul Revere to make the famous Liberty Bowl (now preserved at the MFA).

On September 5, 1774, the First Continental Congress, drawn from all the colonies except Georgia, met at Carpenter's Hall in Philadelphia, where a list of grievances was drawn up and sent to the king.

In mid-December when Revere, a Son of Liberty, learned of General Gage's secret plan to strengthen Fort William and Mary at Portsmouth, he galloped there to alert local patriots Samuel Cutts, John Langdon, and John Sullivan of Durham. These leaders, aided by eager Sons of Liberty, then raided the fort and forced its surrender. During two visits there, the men seized vital powder, cannon, musket, and ball, and carried them by hand through nearly freezing, waist-deep water for transport by gundalow and then by cart to Cambridge for delivery to the militia besieging Boston.[36]

As the Sons of Liberty proliferated throughout the colonies, dissidence increased. In late February 1775, when protests again reached Parliament, Pitt asked his government to remove all British forces from Boston. His request was not approved. Moreover, a bill was introduced forbidding New Englanders to trade in any countries except the West Indies and England, and prohibiting them from fishing in North Atlantic waters. The question then, according to Sir Edmund Burke, was "not whether you have a right to render your people miserable, but whether it is not in your interest to make them happy."

In the cold winter of 1775, old Liberty Tree, from whose branches many hated representatives of the Crown had been hanged in effigy, was at last felled by British soldiers to make fourteen cords of wood for their campfires.

Bunker Hill

After the Lexington and Concord engagements of mid-April 1775, and following a mutually agreed swap of loyalists and rebels into and out of Boston, about forty-five hundred militiamen and volunteers from all over New England left their farms to help tighten a siege ring around the town.

By mid-May, these men were restless; many had already gone home to plant their crops. To keep his remaining volunteers in shape and as a taunt to General Gage, Connecticut's General Israel Putnam[37] marched his war-whooping rebels along the Charlestown shore and over Bunker Hill—despite His Majesty's warships anchored in the Charles.

About a month later—having knowledge that British Generals Howe, Clinton, and Burgoyne, with many additional troops, had arrived aboard the *Cerberus* on May 25 to reinforce Gage, and having also learned of Gage's secret plan to seize Dorchester heights on June 18—the patriots' Committee of Safety hastily decided to occupy Bunker Hill as a diversionary move.

Around noon on the June 16, American siege commander General Artemas Ward and others left Cambridge headquarters on horseback for a strategic look at the Charlestown terrain. His brother-in-arms Colonel William Prescott was then ordered to occupy the hill that same night, deploying around twelve hundred men. At the last moment however, Prescott and his aides decided to defend Breed's Hill instead, so there in the dark a redoubt was begun.

At daybreak on June 17, sleepy Bostonians were jolted from their beds by the boom of cannon from HMS *Lively,* a twenty-gun frigate anchored in the mouth of the Charles.

The astonished British, determined to drive the rebels off, quickly mustered men for a massive assault.

BUNKER HILL MONUMENT.

Although troop movements on Breed's Hill[38] that sultry afternoon were largely hidden by smoke and cinders rising from the blazing ruins of Charlestown, Bostonians went to their rooftops to watch
the awful pageant across the Charles. Twice the regulars climbed to
battle and twice their scarlet ranks[39] were devastated before, at last,
they stormed the height.

General William Howe, a veteran of the French and Indian Wars,
valiantly led the main attack, while Generals Clinton and Pigot lent
him their vigorous support. The rebel redoubt was courageously defended by the patriots and the militia until their powder was ex-
hausted.[40] Today, John Trumbull's famous painting of this historic
climax may be viewed at Yale University. (Trumbull, who served as a
Connecticut militiaman at Bunker Hill, would later serve as an aide
to Washington at Dorchester Heights.)

Meanwhile at Philadelphia on June 15, the Second Continental
Congress,[41] urged by Samuel and John Adams, had commissioned
Colonel George Washington "General of the Continental Army."

Several days later, with Generals Lee and Schuyler, he headed
northward to Cambridge Common where, beneath the famous
Washington Elm, he formally took command of all New England
forces.[42] At headquarters, he received a full report on the recent battle in Charlestown and appointed Israel Putnam to the rank of major
general.[43]

In retrospect, the Breed's Hill battle is viewed as a turning point in
the struggle for independence. New England farm boys, with little
training and poor equipment, had stood up to the regulars; the siege
of Boston had been strengthened, and the colonies were at last awakened and united.[44] Relays of fast riders carried the news all the way to
Georgia, and crack riflemen from the frontiers soon joined Washington's army, bringing their guns.[45] However, in Cambridge, the new
commander was faced with severe problems. He could find only
ninety pounds of gunpowder for his entire northeast army, and was
presented with a local militia unwilling to accept discipline from
Continental officers. Indeed, these same difficulties would plague
him throughout the siege and beyond.

In early October, Benjamin Franklin, with Virginia's Benjamin

Harrison and North Carolina's Thomas Lynch, conferred with General Washington in Cambridge on these pressing obstacles. At least Congress decided to be helpful; by mid-month, it authorized the building of a navy.

Decades passed. Sleepy people in Boston were again jolted from their beds by the boom of cannon at daybreak. It was June 17, 1825, the fiftieth anniversary of the battle of Bunker Hill, and Lafayette had returned. For nearly a year, he had toured the States, visiting old battlefields and friends. Now he came to help New Englanders lay the cornerstone of a monument at their historic hilltop. Daniel Webster, too, was there to address a huge gathering that included veterans of the battle of '75.

Granite for an obelisk designed by Soloman Willard was hauled from the Quincy quarries over one of America's first railroads, and Willard designed a variety of ingenious machines to handle the heavy stones. Laomi Baldwin was his engineer.

Today, the monument's spiraling stone stairway leading to a lookout near the top still offers a handsome view of the Boston skyline, while far below a bronze likeness of patriot William Prescott stands in frozen action near the southern brow of the hill. The extended right hand firmly grips a sword while the left reaches backward in an attitude of restraint consistent with his famous command, "Don't fire until you see the whites of their eyes!"[46] The sculptor was William Storey.

Within the monument museum stands a marble likeness of Dr. Joseph Warren, beloved patriot leader and volunteer soldier, who died in the climax of battle here. Sculptor Henry Dexter has portrayed him clothed in the Roman toga that he wore during his oration at Old South on March 5, 1775. Copley's portrait of Warren now hangs at the MFA.

Dorchester Heights

Dorchester Heights, now Telegraph Hill in South Boston, is an isolated rise commanding a wide view of Boston Harbor, the islands, and Quincy Bay.[47] At its summit stand an eighty-foot white marble tower built in 1902 that reminds New Englanders of a very special day during their struggle for independence.

After the battle at Breed's Hill, the Continental Army worked feverishly to tighten the band of containment around the Boston peninsula. Accordingly, certain outlying hills, groves of trees, stone walls, and bridges became vital to the overall strategy.

By early January of 1776, Washington's plans for a spring offensive were moving steadily forward; engineers Richard Gridley and Rufus Putnam[48] were busy improving fortifications at Lechmere Point and building forts along Dorchester Neck—all as quietly as they could. Then a veiled remark was leaked by a man from a Roxbury camp who said that fascines were being cut to aid in annoying the enemy. (Fascines are tightly bound bundles of sticks that since ancient times have had countless military uses.) Indeed, months of preparation were about to produce a real climax to the long siege of Boston.

In the early morning of March 5, 1776, the sixth anniversary of the Boston Massacre, British general William Howe awoke to find Washington's men firmly established on Dorchester Heights with their cannon posing a threat to the king's occupation forces, his navy, and the vital wharves of Boston! The astonished Howe, appraising the American redoubt with his glass, was quick to comment that the rebels had accomplished more in one night than his whole army could do in months.

The cannon at Dorchester Heights had been captured in May of 1775 by Benedict Arnold and Ethan Allen from British fortresses at Ticonderoga, Crown Point and Fort George.

DORCHESTER HEIGHTS.

In mid-November of the same year, Washington had directed a young civilian, Henry Knox, and his men to bring these guns to Cambridge.[49] After reaching Ticonderoga about mid-December, they had ferried most of the weapons over Lake George. Then, using great teams of oxen and horses, they sledded and dragged their prizes for many grinding days, making several crossings of the Hudson before reaching Albany, and pushing onward through the Berkshires over steep, snow-covered trails to a Continental depot near Framingham. Throughout their long ordeal, the men were cheered by village and country folk who gave them hearty food, overnight lodgings, and other vital supplies.

When at last they reached Cambridge on January 24, 1776, they had covered nearly three hundred miles of rough terrain.

After dark on March 4, as General Howe the next day so unhappily was to discover, the Americans under General Thomas successfully possessed the heights. For three long days, their operations had been disguised by a thick fog, by hay mounded to hide their operations and scattered to quiet the rumble of wagon wheels, by a steady diversionary bombardment from Colonel Knox's cannon on the perimeter of Boston, and by the explosions of answering enemy shells.

In a March 2 letter to her husband, John, Abigail Adams in Braintree wrote her instantaneous impression of that barrage: "But Hark! The house this instant shakes with the roar of cannon."[50]

Although deep frost ruled out the building of conventional earthworks for defending the heights, clever prefabricated fascines of tightly bound brush and straw tied to solid frames were in readiness. An abatis was fashioned from tree limbs, while an array of gravel-filled barrels was triggered to roll upon Howe's redcoats—thus completing a formidable show of strength. Before dawn on the fifth, Thomas's dedicated civilian workers were quite ready to welcome army replacements.

As General Howe's troop carriers were readied for launching that morning and as Washington stood on Dorchester heights reminding his men that this was the anniversary of the Boston Massacre, a sudden severe storm developed. Powerful gusts, often reaching hurricane force, struck the harbor and continued unabated into the next day. Before nightfall on March 6, Howe's initiative was hopelessly lost.[51]

On March 8, a truce signal appeared at the outermost British position on Boston neck.[52] An unaddressed paper signed by four Boston selectmen was then handed to Colonel Leonard for delivery to General Washington. It said Howe was preparing to leave and that he would not harm the town unless he was molested. In Boston that day, merchant John Rowe made an entry in his diary: "Nothing but hurry and confusion, every person striving to get out of this place."

By March 16, the Americans had seized strategic Nook's Hill close to the harbor, thus speeding Howe's departure. Only days earlier, Washington's alternatives had included a risky invasion of the town from the Charles River or over icebound Roxbury Flats. By 9 A.M. on Sunday, March 17, Howe's heavily loaded ships had pulled away from Long Wharf "in a light breeze." By afternoon that day, a thousand men under General Putnam were ferried over the Charles to the foot of the Common to take over the peninsula and the nearby redoubts. Other American troops entered over the neck and through the harbor.[53]

On March 18, Washington, too, entered town and by March 20, families and friends were swarming in for happy reunions. In a letter to his friend, John Hancock, president of the Continental Congress, the general wrote, "I have a particular pleasure in being able to inform you, Sir, that your house has received no damage worth mentioning."[54]

After leaving Long Wharf on the seventeenth, Howe's evacuation fleet, numbering 78 ships and carrying 8,906 soldiers and sailors and about 1,100 Tory refugees, gathered in the outer harbor to adjust cargoes and take on fresh water before setting their sails for Halifax on March 25.

Abigail Adams, watching this historic assemblage from Penn's Hill in Braintree wrote, "We have a view of the largest fleet ever seen in America. You may count upwards of a hundred and seventy sail. They look like a forest."[55]

Although no hostile British forces ever again landed in Boston, some of their ships continued to stand in the outer harbor for several months. These were constantly harassed by the New Englanders. On May 17, the British ship *Hope,* carrying one hundred half-barrels of powder for the now departed General Howe, was captured by Marblehead's James Mugford, commander of the schooner *Franklin.* Mugford turned over his prize to General Ward in Boston, but only two days later Mugford was killed in a naval skirmish while trying to leave the harbor through Shirley Gut.

Boston Light

Since 1716, a lighthouse has guided mariners past a stark pile of rocks, called Little Brewster Island, at the entrance to the outer harbor of Boston. This is one of four similar outcroppings named for Plymouth Plantation's Elder William Brewster when the harbor was explored by Myles Standish in 1621. After the first lighthouse was built, the rocks were known for a while as Beacon Island. Ships entering or leaving the harbor at that time, if engaged in foreign trade, were charged one penny per ton; local shipping paid on a yearly and less costly basis.

The first lighthouse keeper, George Worthylake, knew the islands, rocks, shoals, and channels of the harbor very well; he had been raised on Pemberton Island, he owned a farm on Lovell's Island, and while he kept the lighthouse his sheep grazed on Great Brewster Island only about a quarter mile to the northwest. Still, in early November 1718, while homeward bound from a social outing, Worthylake, his wife Ann, and his daughter Ruth were drowned in a fierce gale while attempting to return in their open boat. Their misfortune was soon immortalized in a ballad written and printed by twelve-year-old Benjamin Franklin, the "Lighthouse Tragedy," which sold readily, although Franklin supposedly later acknowledged it as "wretched stuff."

By 1740, the lighthouse had a guard in constant attendance. When a ship approached, a signal was sent to Castle William at the entrance to the inner harbor. If several suspicious ships appeared at one time, the fort signaled certain people in the town who were always ready to fire the tar bucket on Beacon Hill to warn the populace of danger.

In 1775, when the harbor was blockaded by British ships, possession of Little Brewster Island and its lighthouse shifted several times

BOSTON LIGHT

following fierce engagements and burnings by rebel and British forces. In the spring of 1776, however, the lighthouse was blown to bits by the king's marines during their climatic withdrawal from Boston and its outer harbor.

Today's handsome granite tower was constructed in 1783. Seventy-seven years later its superstructure was raised a little to its current height of ninety-eight feet.

Boston Light is now a national historic landmark.

Federal

(1783–circa 1820)

C-1 New State House   C-2 First Harrison Gray Otis House   C-3 Second Harrison Gray Otis House
C-4 14 Walnut Street   C-5 Saint Stephen's Church   C-6 Amory-Ticknor House   C-7 Nichols House
C-8 Higginson House   C-9 Third Harrison Gray Otis House   C-10 Charles Street Meetinghouse
C-11 54 and 55 Beacon Street   C-12 Hancock Street   C-13 West Church   C-14 Park Street Church

The Federal Era

As America's leaders began their long, often frustrating march toward a federal system of government about a year after a provisional peace agreement was declared in 1783, the lifestyles of most Americans were little changed from colonial days.

Highways were rough, winding, and slow. The drive to push Indian tribes beyond the Appalachians continued, and a majority of the remaining settlers lived off self-sufficient farms within two hundred miles of the Atlantic. Draft animals, waterwheels, and windmills were the main sources of energy; illumination was derived chiefly from whale oil lamps and candles; heat was obtained mainly from wood; and the industrial revolution had barely begun.

But United States history was unfolding, and as the Constitutional Convention led by George Washington opened in Philadelphia on

WENTWORTH GARDNER HOUSE, PORTSMOUTH, N.H.

May 25, 1787, feelings of pride must have surged through the provincial State House, now known as Independence hall.

The Federalist Party, which was born of this gathering, favored the dreams and aims of wealthy shipowners, merchants, industrialists, and large landholders throughout the middle and north Atlantic states. Its time of political strength was short, and Thomas Jefferson, a champion of the common people, skillfully hastened its decline.

Nevertheless, when Washington decided that eight years away from his beloved Mount Vernon were quite enough, the Federalists still were strong enough to elect John Adams president, and to lend their party name to an era of elegant architecture and home furnishings in America.

On March 8, 1797, having attended inaugural ceremonies for President Adams on March 4, Washington and his family departed Philadelphia at 7 A.M. for the return journey to Mt. Vernon.

In September 1800, John Adams became the first president to live in Washington on the Potomac, where he moved from Philadelphia. He and Abigail found many stumps but very few houses there. The president's home, whose cornerstone was laid in 1792, was "a castle of a place" but unfinished; its rooms were sparsely furnished and thirteen fireplaces were needed to make it tolerably warm.[1]

Today, the president's residence is the oldest building standing in the capital. It was officially named the White House by Theodore Roosevelt when he used that name on his stationery. It was first whitewashed in 1798.

In November 1800, a joint session of the House and Senate sat for the first time in the Capitol.

When General Howe evacuated Boston in March of 1776, he precipitated a mass exodus of loyalist merchants and others sympathetic to the Crown. As they fled to Halifax or England, their properties were confiscated by the Continental authorities. A flood of new American leaders then entered Boston to fill the void. They came primarily from maritime communites to the northeast, from which most loyalists had long since fled. Later, as America adjusted to peace, these new leaders became the builders of an industrial expansion that affected the lives of most men and women in New England.

Weary farmers sensed the advantages of a manufacturing occupation, and countless young women left their homes to find employment and independence in textile factories, where often they were offered free courses in social etiquette after the day's work was done. Other women, having more leisure, engaged in beautiful sewing, embroidery, and quilting.

As affluence grew, capable New England architects emerged. Among these were Charles Bulfinch, Asher Benjamin, Peter Banner, and Samuel McIntire, the famous Salem wood-carver. Skilled artisans applied their talents to creations in wood, silver, ivory, copper, and stone.

In 1792, as opulence continued to spread, Boston's town fathers felt able to start burning whale oil street lamps on a regular basis. Previously these had been lighted only in winter or on moonless summer nights.

Designers of Boston's Federal era houses were indebted to the Georgian plans of their earlier English counterparts: Sir William Chambers, Sir John Soane, Sir Christopher Wren, and, still earlier, Inigo Jones, who was an admiring follower of that great sixteenth-century Italian Renaissance student, Andrea Palladio. However, as America's spirit of independence from almost everything English grew, some innovative architects began deserting correct and traditional Georgian styles for the lighter, more graceful, and more elegant classical interpretations of Robert Adam, a Scot, whose maturing work was exciting to the Americans. Adam had visited ancient Mediterranean sites for inspiration, and in 1764 he published his study, *Ruins of the Palace of Diocletian in Dalmatia*. (Today, that walled enclosure at Split still contains Emperor Diocletian's important Roman relics which he acquired mostly by military conquests in Europe and the Middle East.)

As the Federal period advanced, and as prosperity continued to spread through all social levels, many New Englanders who were only moderately well-to-do sought ways to renovate their colonial- or Georgian-style homes to mirror the ever-growing classical revival trends. Their yearnings often were satisfied simply by adding surface symbols of ancient Roman and Greek cultures to the outsides and the insides of their houses. Exterior changes that instantly could convey a sense of affluence might include the use of friezes with triglyph motifs placed below the roof cornices. Palladian windows and fan-lighted doorways were especially desirable, and floor-length windows that opened onto wrought-iron balconies could quickly suggest the splendid neo-classic facades of Paris.

Important inner rooms might be enriched by arched wood-carved doorways and cornices, by plaster castings of floral designs applied to walls and ceilings, and by ornately sculptured fireplace friezes embellished with Greek frets or dentils. Moreover, inlaid marble floors and colorful English and French wallpapers showing Renaissance settings in Naples, Paris, and England were among the choices available to New England designers of the day.

Important British-born cabinetmakers and interior designers who left their mark on this period were Thomas Chippendale, George Hepplewhite, Thomas Sheraton, and Duncan Phyfe.

The Wentworth Gardner House in Portsmouth, New Hampshire, shown above on page 95 was built in 1760. Although later embellished, it is typical of the strong classical influences that still may be seen in New England coastal towns, where handsome mansions were built for successful China trade merchants during the federal period. The wide boards on the front facade are notched and beveled to resemble courses of stone blocks and corner quoins.

Around the start of the nineteenth century, in Salem, a major new American craftsman and architect of the federal era had matured. This was the ingenious Samuel McIntire whose services were so eagerly sought by wealthy local people.

His beautiful three-story mansions and his exquisite wood carvings of cornices, fireplaces, doorways, finials, urns, balustrades, and grapevines still may be seen and enjoyed in Salem and nearby towns. Two of his handsome Salem houses, now open for public viewing, are the Gardner-Pingree House and the Pierce-Nichols House. Both offer excellent examples of his work. In Boston, too, one may view his "Oak Hill rooms" at the MFA.

Although McIntire was a self-taught follower of Robert Adam, his choice and treatment of motifs often were innovative. He had many followers of his style.

The China Venture

During the Revolution, foreign commerce in Boston came to a virtual halt. Then, as the war progressed, Congress encouraged privateering, so ably conducted by John Paul Jones and other fearless American seamen who preyed on enemy shipping throughout the Atlantic. In their insolence, the Americans boldly invaded British coastal waters as well. Still, as time passed, losses from this risky lifestyle mounted.

When peace returned, Boston merchants found their fleets severely weakened and their markets mostly lost. Reciprocal trade with England was discouraged by parliamentary restrictions, and West Indies commerce was banned entirely.

Shipping continued in the doldrums for a time, then revived a little, but not enough to lure the grand old merchant fleets from their harbors. Depressed traders began sniffing the wind for ways to break into the China trade, long denied them by British regulations. About 1784, there appeared a posthumous publication from the journal of the great English explorer and navigator, Capt. James Cook, regarding his exploration of America's northwest coast aboard the *Resolution*. Among the natural wonders that the captain extolled were the hoards of sea otters frolicking in the surf and kelp. By chance, this information dovetailed nicely with Canton reports saying that wealthy mandarins could never have enough sea otter furs! So off around the Horn went eager Boston traders to swap trinkets with the Oregon Indians and collect the needed skins.[2]

In 1784, the earliest American traders bound for China aboard the *Empress of China* reached Whampoa Anchorage on the Pearl River. There, according to supercargo Samuel Shaw, a Bostonian, "[t]hey styled us the New People and when, by the map, we conveyed to them an idea of the extent of our country, they were not a little pleased at the prospect of so considerable a market."

CONJECTURAL VIEW OF THE CHINA VENTURE.

Supercargoes, who were the buyers and sellers during these ventures, later became known as "foreign devils" due to their sharp and questionable business practices. Nevertheless the Americans soon were selling many thousands of sea otter pelts to the Chinese at a huge profit. Clearly, the plundering of American wildlife had begun.

The Boston vessels *Columbia* and *Washington* also carried Pacific sea slugs to the Chinese, who prized them for use in their soups. Shipbuilding boomed; wharves and warehouses mushroomed in New England ports; and young men answered the call of the sea, whether they served as cabin boys or captains. Yankee enterprise returned to life and, as the China trade expanded, East Indies shipping also grew. Many exotic treasures were brought back for American consumption. Very popular were the durable Chinese porcelains, so-called because their glazes so closely resembled the soft sheen on pig-shaped cowrie shells found in Indo-Pacific waters.

Countless tons of such porcelain "ballast" were unloaded at the wharves of Boston, Salem, Portsmouth, and other coastal towns.[3] Before long, it became common for New England trading vessels to circle the globe, loading and unloading at any welcoming port. The great East India Company was soon undersold.

Then, as speed became ever more important in the mid-1830s, the sharp-nosed clipper ships were born. Carrying great clouds of sail, they knifed their way through all the seas for nearly a quarter century. Clippers were brought to perfection by Nova Scotia–born Donald McKay, who built first at Newburyport and later at East Boston, where twenty-one vessels—including *Flying Cloud, Stag Hound, Glory of the Seas, Great Republic,* and *Lightning*—slid down the ways.

Two prominent eastern Massachusetts museums have long displayed fabulous China trade memorabilia. These are the Peabody Museum in Salem and the Museum of the American China Trade in Milton. (In 1984, in Salem, the two collections were merged into one.)

New State House

Before New State House was built on Beacon Hill, many pageants of history were witnessed from that choice high ground whence one could look over the Common, the harbor, the Charles, and Roxbury Flats, part of which is now called Back Bay. Or one could look northward over the peninsula to similar drumlins of glacial drift beyond Charlestown.

In 1737, a handsome mansion was built for the affluent merchant Thomas Hancock on his Beacon Hill pasture. Granite for its walls was cut from surface boulders found in Braintree and sandstone for its trim was quarried in Middletown, Connecticut.

In describing his beloved pasture before the mansion was built, Hancock wrote to his seed supplier in England saying, "My Gardens all Lye on the South Side of a hill with the most beautiful Assent to the top & its allowed on all hands the Kingdom of England don't afford so Fine a Prospect as I have both of land & water."[4]

Following Thomas Hancock's death, the house eventually went to his nephew, John Hancock, merchant, patriot, president of the Second Continental Congress, and, for nine terms, governor of Massachusetts. Over the years, the occupants of this house lavishly hosted patriots, diplomats, allies, prominent world figures, and enemy forces before at last it was taken down in 1863.

In 1793, after Governor Hancock died, his widow sold about two acres near the garden to the town of Boston. The town then quickly resold the land to the state for five shillings, historians say, and thus a site for the new state house was assured.

Charles Bulfinch's proposed design was accepted, and by July 4, 1795, the exterior construction was about to begin.

At an official gathering that included several Indian chiefs, fifteen white horses representing the fifteen states drew the cornerstone up

NEW STATE HOUSE.

the hill. Paul Revere, as Grand Master of the Grand Lodge of Masons, officially laid the first stone of this handsome state house, built of red brick and trimmed with white marble. Gov. Samuel Adams and Mr. Revere delivered addresses, and the governor was returned to Old State amidst cheers and booming cannon.

The interior plans for New State suggest the restrained elegance of Robert Adam and other English designers of the time, but they are rich with classical innovations in the finest Bulfinch style.

Gold leaf was applied to the dome in 1874, and ever since, on sunny days, a warm glow has shone from Beacon Hill, except for a time during World War II when the dome was camouflaged.

First Harrison Gray Otis House

T his late-Georgian-style red-brick house, standing near West Church, is the first of three designed for Harrison Gray Otis by his friend and associate, Charles Bulfinch. It was built in 1797.

FIRST HARRISON GRAY OTIS HOUSE.

Otis, a lawyer, was a nephew of patriot James Otis and an able orator in his own right. As a New England Federalist, he captained a Boston company of light infantry against Shays' Rebellion in 1787. Starting in 1797, his record of public service is impressive: he was twice a state legislator; once a United States representative; once a United States senator; and last, in 1829, a mayor of Boston.

As an old man, Otis wrote of the momentous morning of April 19, 1775. He was ten years old and Tremont Street was filled with Lord Percy's reinforcement troops preparing to march on Lexington and Concord.[5] Even so, Otis reported dutifully at the Boston Latin School. But Mr. Lovell, the master, said, "War's come; school's done; put aside your books."[6]

In 1916, Otis' Cambridge Street house was acquired by the Society for the Preservation of New England Antiquities. Currently, it houses a fine research library, an excellent museum with rooms furnished in the bright and airy atmosphere of comfortable federal era interiors, and the offices of the society.

Otis's 1804 portrait by Gilbert Stuart hangs in the dining room of this house.

The Frigate *Constitution*

The frigate *Constitution* (commonly known as *Old Ironsides*), now moored at Charlestown navy Yard, was built by Edmund Hartt at "Hartt's Naval Yard" near Constitution Wharf. She was launched in 1791 and was designed to carry forty-four cannon but often supported fifty-two. Today, these guns still are known by such affectionate names as Polly, Jumping Billy, Rattlesnake, and Willful Murder.

For his fine work, Hartt was awarded a silver tea service designed by Paul Revere, whose company supplied most of the copper and

THE FRIGATE *CONSTITUTION*

brass work needed for this ship. She saw action in the Tripolitan War against the Barbary pirates in the early 1800s and against the British in the War of 1812, during which she fought several victorious battles, earning the name *Old Ironsides.* One of the most memorable of her commanders was Capt. Isaac Hull of Connecticut, whose superior seamanship on August 19, 1812, helped sink the British warship *Guerriere* in one of the most furious encounters of the war. At last, however, she was declared unseaworthy and condemned. But Oliver Wendell Holmes, at age twenty-eight, wrote his famous poem, *Old Ironsides,* to arouse America and effect a restoration in 1833. For a time, the *Constitution* served as a naval training ship. She was restored again by donations from schoolchildren in 1925, and a major overhaul was completed in 1975. Today, she is the oldest commissioned warship still afloat, and she continues to be staffed by United States naval officers and sailors who welcome the public aboard.

Nearby stands the *Constitution* Museum, a granite building designed by Alexander Parris, where many interesting artifacts and reminders of *Old Ironsides's* maritime history may be seen. The *Constitution* is probably the most famous ship in United States naval history.

Second Harrison Gray Otis House

In 1774, about two decades after artist John Singleton Copley moved permanently to England, eleven acres of his seventeen-acre Beacon Hill farm were sold to Harrison Gray Otis, Jonathan Mason, Charles Bulfinch, and other members of a land-developing group known as the Mount Vernon Proprietors. Adjacent acreage, including mudflats to the west, also was purchased by the company until it owned lands which today would be bounded roughly by Beacon, Joy, Pinckney, and Charles Streets.

Copley regretted his land sale, feeling that his agent had acted without full authority. Nevertheless, he failed to recover the farm.[7]

Boston was entering an era of expansion and prosperity; a new state house would soon add stature to Beacon Hill, where property would be highly prized by successful merchants, bankers, shipbuilders, and others.

In 1802, Otis built his second red-brick Georgian-style mansion on the south brow of Beacon Hill. This is now known as 85 Mount Vernon Street. It was even more elegant than his first handsome Georgian home on Cambridge Street. Charles Bulfinch designed both.

The Mount Vernon Proprietors were indeed astute businessmen. Undoubtedly they set the stage for a certain quality of living long associated with Beacon Hill.

SECOND HARRISON GRAY OTIS HOUSE.

14 Walnut Street

hen Dr. Joy, for whom Joy Street was named, decided to sell a part of his Beacon Hill garden land to John Callender for a house lot, he mentioned his decision to a friend, so the story goes, saying that Callender wanted to build a "small house for very little money."[8] Callender then built this not exactly modest wood-framed house with brick ends in 1802.

A VIEW OF
14 WALNUT STREET

St. Stephen's Church

This fine old church, built of red brick on Hanover Street, was designed by Charles Bulfinch and was erected in 1804. It faces Revere Mall and Cyrus Dallin's bronze likeness of patriot Revere astride his galloping horse.[9] Beyond the statue rises the spire of Christ Church. St. Stephen's is now the only remaining Bulfinch church in the Old Hub, and is considered to represent the finest Bulfinch style inside and out.

ST. STEPHEN S CHURCH.

Amory-Ticknor House

The late-Georgian-style red-brick house standing at the head of Park Street was built for merchant Thomas Amory in 1804. Its designer was Charles Bulfinch. Because Amory soon suffered financial reverses it was called Amory's Folly and for a while it served as a guest house. Christopher Gore lived here for a time during his term as governor.

AMORY-TICKNOR HOUSE.

General Lafayette,[10] who was invited to America by President Monroe, made this house his headquarters while stopping in Boston in late August 1824. He was received, paraded, and entertained by mayor Josiah Quincy, and from the balcony of this house he greeted his many admirers. Great throngs filled the streets to give the old soldier a hero's welcome. Although the day was cold, he constantly bared his head to acknowledge the cheering crowds; this prompted the mayor to comment later that it was fortunate Lafayette wore a wig. The general's companion during this visit was his son, George Washington Lafayette.

During his stay at Amory House, the marquis was driven on Sunday, August 29, to Quincy, where he dined with former President John Adams. Lafayette found his old friend surrounded by his family and still alert at eighty-nine. They exchanged many memories.[11]

At a later time, part of Amory House was used by George Ticknor, a popular Harvard professor of languages, who today is admired by scholars for his monumental *History of Spanish Literature*. Most of Ticknor's thirteen thousand volume library, once located in a room overlooking the Common, is preserved now at the Boston Public Library, which he helped to found.

Ticknor's oil portrait by Thomas Sully hangs at the Hood Museum of Art, Dartmouth College.

Nichols House

In 1804, Jonathan Mason built this red-brick house at 55 Mount Vernon Street for his daughter. Although its design is typical of Charles Bulfinch, some think it was the work of Asher Benjamin.

From 1880 to 1960, it was the home of Rose Nichols, a woman dedicated to promoting better understanding among the world's peoples. She was an ardent collector of antiques and a student of landscape architecture, about which she wrote several books. Her house was willed as a public museum and is opened for public viewing on certain days of each week.

NICHOLS HOUSE.

Higginson House

This late-Georgian house at 87 Mount Vernon Street was planned by Charles Bulfinch about 1805. Some believe Bulfinch originally built the house for himself. Nevertheless, he sold it to Stephen Higginson, a Boston merchant.

HIGGINSON HOUSE.

Third Harrison Gray Otis House

Before long, Otis tired of his second mansion and bought a new site on Beacon Street. According to local legend, he vowed he would never part with this land even though a willing buyer might offer gold doubloons sufficient to pave the whole property one inch deep; nor did he do so.

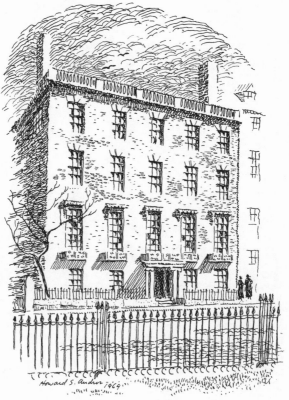

THIRD HARRISON GRAY OTIS HOUSE.

Here in 1806, Otis built his third and most sumptuous red-brick home, now 45 Beacon Street, where he could enjoy a fine view over the waters of Back Bay and onward to the Blue Hills of Milton. Again, Bulfinch was his designer.

At first, it was a freestanding house with an outward-curving wall on its upper side enclosing a ballroom. On the lower side today, a cobblestoned driveway leads to a side door or to a stable. In his later years, Otis often sat in an east window of his library to watch the flow of people, wagons, and carriages on Beacon Street and the children playing on the Common.

In 1806, the family's social presence in Boston was secure. Formal parties, dancing, exotic foods, and rare wines were offered in this home, with restrained but elegant New England taste, amid comfortable surroundings aglow with whale oil lamps and candles.

Here, on Thanksgiving Day, 1817, Otis was host to President Monroe.

Charles Street Meeting House

This red-brick meetinghouse standing at the foot of Mount Vernon Street was designed by Asher Benjamin and completed about 1807. When it was built, for Baptists, it stood at the edge of a tidal estuary of the Charles. Although the water has long been displaced by landfill, the area retains its old name, Back Bay."

Benjamin's basic design for this building is similar to his plan for West Church on Cambridge Street. Far less surface ornamentation is employed at Charles Street, but elegant, recessed brick arches are used more liberally.

Despite inner changes, the building's nineteenth-century shell, interior columns and arches, and coffered ceiling have been saved.

CHARLES STREET MEETING HOUSE.

54 and 55 Beacon Street

These houses were co-designed by Asher Benjamin and James Coburn, the Boston merchant for whom they were built in 1808. They reflect a period of transition in building styles; a

A VIEW OF 54 AND 55 BEACON STREET.

departure from the symmetry and classical purity of earlier Georgian designs was underway on Beacon Hill. Regency bowfronts and Greek Revival trends were on the rise. During this interval, granite, sandstone, and sometimes marble were used for facings, steps, gateposts, and other accessories. But New England architects of the day were hardly limited to the use of stone. In outlying towns, wood, being plentiful, often was fashioned to resemble stone.

Hancock Street

As prosperity increased in New England during the first half of the nineteenth century, the upper middle class, forever seeking ways to emulate the well-to-do, but rarely able to pay for costly hand-wrought exterior ironwork, eagerly joined an emerging trend which favored mass-produced cast-iron substitutes. Balconies, fences, gateways, and balustrades depicting such Mediterranean flora

HANCOCK STREET.

as the acanthus and the double anthemion, in recurring themes, soon became cast-iron musts for many downtown Boston dwellings.

Hancock Street passes through the site of Thomas Hancock's estate, which became the home of his son, John Hancock. Hancock House was demolished in 1863. Hancock Street is now home to many fine homes in the Federal, Greek Revival, and Egyptian Revival styles, some with elaborate cast-iron balconies and railings.

Among early proponents of cast-iron embellishments were Robert Adam and Asher Benjamin; the latter's guidebooks for builders show designs identical to many of the castings seen today on Beacon Hill.

West Church

West Church, the red-brick building standing next to the Harrison Gray Otis House on Cambridge Street, was designed by Asher Benjamin and completed about 1809.

In 1892, church services were discontinued, but the building was saved by Andrew Wheelwright, who bought the property and held it until the city took it over for a public library.

In 1960, as plans for urban renewal began, the building was considered for possible demolition. It was saved again when Methodist services began about 1965. A banneret vane still whirls above the dome. Today, the church is known as Old West Church.

Asher Benjamin is now widely recognized as the designer of numerous handsome village houses and churches throughout New England, and for his many books published to aid carpenters, builders, and cast-iron craftsmen.

WEST CHURCH.

The Leveling of Beacon Hill and Other Growing Pains

I n 1684, after reports reached Boston that a Privy Council committee in London had ordered a recall of the Massachusetts Bay Colony's charter,[12] a spirit of independence began to show in Boston. Fortifications sprouted at Fort Hill, Castle Island,[13] Dorchester, and Charlestown. A sixty-five-foot tar-bucket beacon was raised on Sentry Hill, where a continuous watch was kept to warn the town of danger.

The natural hills of Boston and Charlestown were formed by glacial movements bringing mixtures of clay, sand, and gravel from the north. As time passed, these deposits were shaped by erosion and gradually reduced. Even so, as the eighteenth century drew to a close, the steep, windblown peak of Beacon Hill stood nearly sixty feet higher than it does today. Indeed, historians have visible proof that before the Revolution ended, the hills of the Boston peninsula were far more formidable than today.

In the summer of 1773, a watercolor painting was executed by British lieutenant William Pierie, who set up his easel amid open farm fields divided by low hedgerows. In the middle foreground of the artist's composition stands Shirley Place, the Roxbury estate of William Shirley, seventh royal governor of the Province of Massachusetts Bay, whose handsome Georgian-style house with its hipped roof and cupola is easily identified in Pierie's landscape. In the distance, beyond Roxbury Flats, spreads the precipitous peninsula of Boston, including the tar-bucket beacon in its usual place atop Beacon Hill.

Only two years later, a fortified British redoubt would occupy the site. Much later, after the Revolution, the beacon pole came down and a Doric column of Bulfinch design was erected in its place. On

A CONJECTURAL VIEW OF THE LEVELING OF BEACON HILL.

its pedestal were slate tablets engraved to recall America's struggle for independence, and atop the brick and stucco column turned a gilded American eagle weather vane carved from wood.

As the nineteenth century opened, a superb panorama still could be enjoyed from the summit of Beacon Hill, where young boys rolled their balls and carried out their pretended military assaults. But the town was expanding and need for landfill was great. From the start of excavations in 1808, nearly a quarter century was required to move the peaks of Boston's several hills by cart and tram to Mill Pond and Back Bay. In summer, local children leaped and rolled from the crests of man-made cuts, and in winter they coasted down the icy steeps on homemade sleds.

When at last Bulfinch's column, too, came down, the tablets were saved, and later remounted on a similar shaft erected far below the original site. This column stands behind New State House today.

In an 1811 letter to Dr. Apthorp, Charles Bulfinch expressed the feelings of naturalists of all eras when he wrote about Old Beacon Hill having been taken down in order to fill in Mill Pond since Governor Hancock's heirs valued utility and "interest" above "elegance." Bulfinch at that time owned property on the back side of Beacon Hill.

In 1814, the legislature accepted Uriah Cotting's proposition to build a mile and a half shortcut roadway starting at the foot of Beacon Hill and crossing scenic Back Bay to Brookline. This roadway is now known as Beacon Street. As an added inducement, the engineer's plans called for installing watergates in the Milldam Road to harness tidal energy.

In July 1821, the roadway at last was opened to traffic, but soon local people were furious about the intermittent lake behind the dam: instead of a natural shoreline of sweet-smelling tidal grasses that surged each spring to hide the nesting waterfowl only to break down and nourish the oysters and the clams, they had an unpredictable water level that perpetually reeked of sewage. It was called the "Back Bay Nuisance."

Nevertheless, entrenched water-powered mills proved difficult to dislodge, and over a half century of political procrastination passed before Back Bay was landfilled as we know it today.

Park Street Church

The handsome red-brick church at Park and Tremont Streets stands on land once occupied by a huge four-story warehouse known as Old Granary, where grain was stored for the poor of the town.

PARK STREET
CHURCH.

Inevitably, however, the rodent population increased and the grain was moved to safer quarters. Later Old Granary proved useful to a sailmaker, and sails for Old Ironsides were cut and sewn there. Still later, to make room for the church, Old Granary was moved to Dorchester and remodeled as a hotel.

Since 1810, Park Street Church has provided one of the most impressive sights in Boston, both from the upper reaches of the Common and throughout the length of Lafayette Mall. Soldiers, sailors, sweethearts, and tourists often use the church as a background for their snapshots. Peter Banner was the designer and Solomon Willard carved the simple capitals above the frontal columns.

Still spinning above the graceful spire is an eight-foot banneret weather vane, the Whopper, installed in 1859. It weighs ninety pounds and on its tail is an exploding star of gilded bronze. On very hot summer days, people downtown watch it closely for the first hint of a cooling east wind from the sea—and with good reason: Bunker Hill Monument reaches only four feet higher.

Park Street Church is central to many interesting aspects of downtown Boston; not the least of these are the historic landmarks that surround it. At the top of Park Street stands Amory-Ticknor House, with Bulfinch's State House just beyond; to the southeast stand the Grecian pediment and columns of St. Paul's; to the south spreads the ancient Common with its pigeon feeders, its folk singers, the Brewer Fountain, and Augustus Saint-Gaudens's bronze relief for Shaw's Memorial; to the north lies Old Granary Burial Ground, a resting place of the patriots.

Greek Revival

(circa 1820–1850)

GREEK REVIVAL PERIOD
1820-1850

N

Charles River

CHARLES RIVER DAM

To Charlestown, Bunker Hill
Monument and "Old Ironsides"

Boston Harbor

U.S. Coast Guard Station

CONSTITUTION WHARF
BATTERY WHARF
LINCOLN'S WHARF
UNION WHARF
SARGENT'S WHARF
LEWIS WHARF
COMMERCIAL WHARF
LONG WHARF
CENTRAL WHARF
INDIA WHARF
ROWE'S WHARF
FOSTER'S WHARF

Copp's Hill

NORTH STATION

Causeway

Blossom St.

Merrimac St.

Chardon St.

Canal St.

Stanford St.

New St.

Sudbury

No.Washington St.

Expressway

Hull St.

Salem St.

Hanover St.

North St.

Commercial St.

Natural Shoreline

(D-3)

Fruit St.

To Cambridge

Cambridge St.

GOVERNMENT CENTER

Jov St.

Hancock St.

Bowdoin St.

Union St.

Dock Sq.

(D-4) South Market St.

Court St.

State St. (D-6)

India St.

Atlantic Avenue

West Cedar St.

(D-7)

Derne St.

Pinckney St.

Mt. Vernon St.

Acorn St.

Chestnut St.

(D-1)

Beacon St.

(D-8)

School St.

Bromfield St.

POST OFFICE

Milk St.

Fort Hill Sq.

Park St.

Tremont St.

PUBLIC GARDEN

The Lagoon

Charles St.

Natural Shoreline

Frog Pond

BOSTON COMMON

(D-2)

Washington St.

Summer St.

Kingston St.

Congress St.

Fort Point Channel

Burying Ground

To Brookline

Boylston St.

Street Pattern in 1995

Essex St.

To South Boston

SOUTH STATION

0   1/10   2/10   3/10
miles

D-1 David Sears House   D-2 Saint Paul's Cathedral   D-3 Massachusetts General Hospital

D-4 Quincy Market   D-5 Granite Warehouses   D-6 Custom House   D-7 Louisburg Square

D-8 10 ½ Beacon

The Greek Revival Era

During the first quarter of the nineteenth century, as more arch-aeological excavations and studies were carried out in Greece and on its far-flung islands, a new era of architecture emerged to spread throughout Europe and America. Undoubtedly this trend was strengthened by worldwide admiration for the Greek people during their fight for independence from the Turks. In America, though, this movement became pandemic: many homes built in colonial or Georgian style were altered to resemble the Parthenon.

Pedimented porticos supported by correctly proportioned Grecian columns of stone or wood portrayed the very essence of stability for banks, courthouses, libraries, churches, and comfortable mansions. They still do. But conservative New England villages were often slow to embrace this trend, so it is in these settlements that the purest forms of colonial and early Georgian styles still may be found. However, overlaps of Federal period plans with Greek Revival symbols are prevalent throughout the Atlantic seaboard states today.

Among national landmarks probably known to New England designers of that time are Thomas Jefferson's state capitol at Richmond; his beloved Monticello begun in 1770; and his University of Virginia, which opened about 1825.[1] These and other Jefferson plans reveal his innovative mind and the influences of his years in France, where he succeeded Franklin as minister in 1785. The French had already altered Paris to reflect the Classical Revival era, and Jefferson, in four years, had ample opportunity to study the results. His Richmond plan was inspired by the Maison Carrée, an ancient Roman ruin at Nîmes in southern France, built by Emperor Augustus for his grandsons.

Other transitional creations were Major L'Enfant's street plan for the "Federal City," requested by George Washington in 1789—but

QUINCY MARKET AND THE EAST END OF FANEUIL HALL.

not carried out until 1901—and the President's home, designed by James Hoban using brown Virginia sandstone, which was later whitewashed. Following the War of 1812, Thornton, Latrobe, Bulfinch, and others drew plans for the restoration of the devastated Capitol, a casualty of the war.[2]

Then came the breathtaking, nearly pure Greek temple design of William Strickland for his twin-porticoed Second Bank of the United States, built at Philadelphia in 1824, and T. U. Walter's Andalusia, high on the banks of the Delaware, which was designed about that time for financier Nicholas Biddle. Biddle's inspiration for his lovely home was the Temple of Poseidon at Paestum, Italy.[3]

In Boston, outstanding planners of the Greek revival period were Alexander Parris, Ammi B. Young, Solomon Willard, and Isaiah Rogers. Bulfinch too was carried on the Greek Revival tide, as shown by his design for Massachusetts General Hospital.

But the flood of Grecian trends in America was not limited to architecture; young women in long, flowing, high-waisted gowns became Greek goddesses on Boston streets. Their hairstyles suggested the ringlet-covered heads of Greek maidens depicted on unearthed murals and mosaics found in ancient Greek and Roman ruins. Moreover, towns throughout America were renamed Athens, Troy, Syracuse, Ithaca, Sparta, and Corinth.

As the Greek Revival era waxed, many hardscrabble New Englanders still were engaged in the two occupations that only they knew so well: shipbuilding, and foreign and domestic trade. As time passed, Boston merchants demanded better inland transportation for their goods. Improved turnpikes brought greater speed and comfort for wagon and coach travel, but canals seemed more promising for freight. One horse on a towpath might haul a load that demanded ten four-horse teams on the roadways.[4]

In 1793, Governor Hancock signed legislation for building the Middlesex Canal, which began operations in 1803. Starting in Charlestown and joining the Merrimac River just above Lowell, barges delivered clothing, spices, and other merchandise as far inland as Concord, New Hampshire, and then returned with lumber and farm harvests for the Boston market. This waterway proved a real bonanza for farmers, loggers, and Boston merchants, but the costs of building and maintaining a 27-mile canal and lock system, involving a rise of 107 feet to the Merrimac, were shocking indeed to the original investors, who received no dividends for 15 years. In fact, by 1833 the railroads threatened to eclipse the canal.[5]

When the heartland of America was linked to the port of New York by the Erie Canal in 1825,[6] Boston merchants, fearing the worst, began surveys for a competitive canal system westward over the Berkshires to the Hudson; but legislators were wary. Then in 1826, when engineer Gridley Bryant built a horse-powered four-mile railroad to haul granite from the Quincy quarries to barges on the shore in order to build the Bunker Hill Monument, the legislators took notice.

By March of 1834, tracks were laid across Back Bay to Newton. Then, despite a delay in the arrival of a steam engine driver from England, a locomotive at last was put to work on April 4 hauling gravel, and three days later a party of over fifty people took the trial run to Davis's Tavern in Newton.

By May 12, a passenger schedule for three daily trips was published in the *Daily Advertiser*. The fare was 37½ cents either way.

By 1835, the Meteor hauled cars as far west as Worcester, which reputedly prompted a Boston shipping agent to call this run "a forty mile extension of Long Wharf." By then, other lines using steam power had reached Providence and Lowell.

In 1842, the Western, an extension of the Boston and Worcester Railroad, climbed over the Berkshires to the Hudson to forge a link between Long Wharf and the western shores of Lake Superior!

As New Englanders neared the middle of the nineteenth century, they proved to be much the same restless, striving, irrepressible people as their immigrant ancestors. The pace of transportation, science, industry, and communication was quicker, and in 1841 Samuel F. B. Morse, a Charlestown native and a capable portrait painter, showed Congress that it was possible to transmit a message in code over a wire stretching between Washington and Baltimore.

Ninety-two years earlier, other inventors already had used electricity as a tool. At that time, Boston-born Benjamin Franklin and his friends had met for a picnic on the banks of the Schuykill River, near

Philadelphia. There, they electrocuted a turkey and turned it on an electrically operated spit over a fire ignited by an electric spark. During the 1840s, many adventurous New England families streamed westward to establish homesteads and tame the prairies, as wave upon wave of English, Irish, and Scottish immigrant replacements were welcomed by eastern America's expanding railroads, factories, and mills. Other New Englanders, however, chose to gamble on a bountiful harvest from the sea. Although Atlantic coast harpooners had speared sperm whales in local New England waters since 1720, by the 1840s a craving for clean-burning sperm oil illumination had so accelerated that whaling fleets sailed from Nantucket and New Bedford to round the Horn and stalk their prey in the Pacific. Such voyages, always dangerous, might last five years, but the profits could be enormous. In 1849, many Bostonians bought tickets to sail around the Horn and join the worldwide stampede for California gold.

David Sears House

O n May 16, 1783, when word reached Boston that a provisional peace treaty[7] had been signed in Paris, prices of foreign merchandise fell rapidly. Notice was published in the *Independent Chronicle* that one David Sears was offering items for sale at his store on State Street at "Peace Prices."

Later, as oriental markets became attractive, Sears joined Elias Hasket Derby of Salem and other local merchants on trading journeys to

DAVID SEARS HOUSE.

the East Indies. Because such early ventures from New England to the Orient were long and expensive, it was commonplace for local merchants to combine their resources and share the risks.

Sears seems to have prospered, for in 1819 this house, designed by Alexander Parris, was built for the merchant at what is now 42 Beacon Street. It was made of Quincy granite, and the marble tablets set in its front wall were carved by Solomon Willard, the designer of Bunker Hill Monument. As originally built, the house had only one bow on the street facade; a second bow was added in 1832.

Much earlier, the home of John Singleton Copley had stood on this spot.

St. Paul's Cathedral

On Tremont Street, not far below Park Street, stands St. Paul's. It was designed by Alexander Parris. Solomon Willard carved the handsome Ionic frontal capitals and columns, and assembled them in Greek style using drums of varying thickness. Quincy granite was used to face the main structure, but the whole portico was finished in richly colored Acquia Greek sandstone found in Virginia. Over the years this material has offered poor resistance to weather, but many people feel that the resulting erosions add only charm and mellowness to the whole effect.

St. Paul's was completed in 1820.

ST. PAUL'S CATHEDRAL.

Massachusetts General Hospital

This handsome Greek revival hospital building, made of Chelmsford granite, stands off Fruit Street on land earlier known as Prince's Pasture. Before extensive landfilling changed the natural shoreline, the Charles River had flowed close by the west walls.

MASSACHUSETTS GENERAL HOSPITAL.

In keeping with the facade, the foyer is simply and beautifully designed. It has a granite slab floor and winding granite slab stairs. This was Bulfinch's last Boston design. In 1818, President Monroe called him to Washington to succeed Latrobe in restoring the Capitol, burned by the British four years earlier.[8] But Bulfinch's Washington stint became a twelve-year engagement, so Alexander Parris was drafted to supervise construction of the hospital, which was finished in 1821 with the help of convict labor. Here, twenty-five years later, ether was first used successfully in a surgical operation.

Charles Bulfinch was innovative and self-taught. He usually is acknowledged as the foremost New England architect of his time.[9] His maternal grandfather was the illustrious King Street merchant Charles Apthorp. His paternal grandfather and his father were physicians. Charles was born in 1763, soon after the close of the French and Indian Wars, so his childhood memories included the Boston Massacre, the Tea Party, the actions at Lexington and Concord, and the Battle at Breed's Hill, which he watched from the roof of his boyhood home in Bowdoin Square.

At age twenty-six in the spring of 1789, Bulfinch took his bride, the former Hannah Apthorp, to New York to attend George Washington's inaugural ceremonies at Federal Hall.[10]

Many of the handsome buildings designed by Bulfinch eventually became victims of urban growth. Still, Massachusetts General Hospital has survived to mark the close of his epochal Boston career. Bulfinch died in 1844 at age eighty-one.

Quincy Market

Soon after the colony was established, an open-air market was conducted every Thursday at what is now the head of State Street. When the wood-framed Town House was built there in 1657, an open but sheltered market was held on the ground floor. Later, after the Town House was consumed by the great fire of 1711, other markets developed. An open-air enterprise was operating in Dock Square when Faneuil Hall was built there in 1742.

THREE VIEWS (PAGES 143–145) OF QUINCY MARKET.

By the 1820s, when growing Boston needed more public buildings, young architects found the Grecian look exciting. They were
lucky; a ready supply of granite was available across the harbor in
Braintree and Quincy. Tidal land just east of Faneuil Hall was chosen
as the site for a new market building, and there in 1825 a cornerstone
was laid. Then, under the untiring direction of Boston's second
mayor, Josiah Quincy, construction was begun and pressed forward
apace.

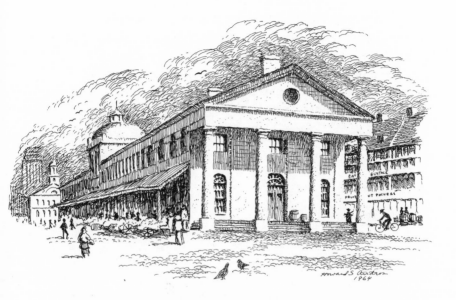

In 1827, when the new building first opened its doors, the inner harbor reached nearly to its east end.

Today the great monolithic columns of its identical porticoes still are exciting to architects and engineers. This venerable 555-foot market, designed by Alexander Parris, is faced with granite slabs and lined with red bricks.

Gilbert Stuart's painting of Josiah Quincy and his market, given by his daughter, Eliza Susan Quincy, now hangs at the MFA.[11]

As late as the 1920s, horse-drawn trucking was commonplace at the market. On an average summer day at noon, a weary trucker might tether Nellie at the curb with an iron hitching weight, put on her straw bonnet and feed bag, and climb the narrow stairs to Durgin Park's. There, at a long table, he would rub elbows with office clerks, bankers, meat handlers wearing long white coats and ancient "straw-boaters," and a mix of unclassifiable gourmets, all revelling in such mouth-watering fare as johnnycake, baked scrod, pot roast, Indian pudding,[12] strawberry shortcake, and apple pandowdy.

The massive granite slab sidewalks; the sounds of horses and carts on cobbled streets; the smells of coffee, spices, vegetables, and fruits; the shouts of vendors; and the bargaining of customers were still very much a part of Quincy Market a century after it was built.

As a part of an urban renewal effort in Boston during the 1970s, this building and its companions, North and South Markets, were renovated to form a downtown shopping mall.

The Granite Warehouses

The builders of Bunker Hill Monument and Quincy Market, using local granite and Greek Revival styles, had shown the way to a new era in Boston architecture. By the mid-1830s, new tools for cutting and shaping stone, and improved methods of

FOUR VIEWS (PAGES 147–150) OF THE GRANITE WAREHOUSES.

transporting it, were welcomed by the builders of stone-faced water-front warehouses in Boston. Because tidal land adjacent to the inner harbor was desirable, construction of underwater foundations for such buildings required the use of wooden diving bells for driving pilings by hand into the heavy blue clay of the harbor floor. A prominent warehouse designer of that time was the self-taught Isaiah Rogers, whose services were in demand in Boston and throughout eastern America.

Later, after the Civil War, commerce at the inner harbor began a slow decline. Merchant fleets, finding the old wharves inadequate, soon moved across the harbor to East Boston. Railroads, too, were cramped by a narrow waterfront crowded with horse-drawn traffic. Eventually, the wharves became useful only to coastal traders and the fishing industry.

Repeated attempts were made to revive the area but all failed. Eventually the old stone warehouses became little more than great hulks, but their removal posed a costly problem. By that quirk of fate, many have survived. More recently, developers have come to recognize their value for apartment living, waterfront shops, business offices, and restaurants with a nautical flavor. Thus many aspects of the harbor's "granite era" have been saved—at least for the present.

Surviving warehouses include: Commercial Block, Commercial Wharf in two parts, Lewis Wharf, Union Wharf, Custom House Block, and Mercantile Buildings. Some of these still stand at the old wharves. Others, because of landfilling, are located now farther inland. Leisure boaters and fishermen still tie their painters to the old piers, and anglers from nine to ninety still bait their hooks and cast their lines there.

Custom House

The Custom House stands at India and State Streets, not far from Quincy Market. Only parts remain of Ammi B. Young's original creation—a stunning, low-domed neoclassical building that dominated the waterfront near the Custom House dock. It

TWO VIEWS (PAGES 151–152) OF THE CUSTOM HOUSE.

was so close to the harbor that the bowsprits of the merchantmen reached almost to its east windows. It was generally considered by all who saw it to be the finest example of Greek revival architecture ever seen in Boston.

Tidal land had been acquired, and starting in 1837 great chains of oxen hauled granite for columns, facings, and ornaments from the Quincy quarries. Although three years were required to prepare the foundations alone, construction was finished ten years after it began.

In 1910, as space seemed limited, a tower of slightly Venetian design was begun above the dome. By 1915, it reached 370 feet above the street and became Boston's first skyscraper. For nearly a half century, it would prevail as the most prominent landmark for returning sailors, and as a reassuring sight for landlubbers lost in the ancient web of narrow downtown streets and alleys.

Louisburg Square

This unique old square, lying on the south slope of Beacon Hill between Mount Vernon and Pinckney Streets, was at one time a part of first settler Blackstone's farm. Nearby bubbled his ample spring.

THREE VIEWS (PAGES 153–155) OF LOUISBURG SQUARE.

During British occupation days, Gage's cannon aimed at Cambridge were emplaced near here.

Although most of the houses in the square were not erected before the 1840s, the design was conceived in 1826, when people on Beacon Hill still could look over the waters of Back Bay, which were broken only by the Milldam Road.

Today, the Greek revival and regency periods of architecture have left lasting impressions on the square, as they have on most of the hill.

The tree-shaded central green, still enclosed by an 1844 iron fence, has long been owned and cared for by the residents who live around the square. One of the early inhabitants presented the green with a

small statue of Aristides, which still may be seen at the lower end. A likeness of Columbus was added later by residents of the upper end. At one time, Louisa May Alcott lived at number ten.

10½ Beacon

In 1805, fourteen local men met in Boston to form an anthology club. Two years later, the club became a privately owned corporation called the Boston Athenaeum. It flourished, and by 1827 its book collection, donated by the members, had grown so large that it was moved to a Pearl Street building offered by James Perkins, a successful merchant in the Java and China trade.

The new quarters had ample space for an art gallery, too, but eventually the library outgrew that building. In 1847, a new three-story brownstone building, designed by Edward Clarke Cabot and George Dexter, was begun at today's Athenaeum site. In 1870, to relieve overcrowding again, the library joined with Harvard and the Massachusetts Institute of Technology (M.I.T.) to create the Museum of Fine Arts, which opened at Copley Square six years later. Then the Athenaeum loaned many of its art treasures to the museum.

In 1913, as the newest Athenaeum became cramped, two more floors designed by Henry Bigelow were built above the original structure. In the finished work, Bigelow chose to use more classical symbols than had the earlier designers. His handsome fifth floor reading room, for example, is capped by a barrel-vaulted ceiling accented with shallow coffers reminiscent of the Pantheon in Rome.

Today, Athenaeum members may look southward through tall French windows to the meandering lines of Old Granary's slate headstones, and beyond to the north facade of Park Street Church with its soaring steeple, or eastward to the old Province Steps and Gateway.

Besides the famed book treasures of this library, which include hundreds of volumes owned by George Washington and John Quincy Adams, this comfortable cloister contains a matchless gallery of busts and statues. Throughout the building these decorative sculptures seem to gaze from wall niches, from pedestals standing

A VIEW OF 10½ BEACON STREET.

around and the reading rooms, and, in fact, from anywhere that such figures would not constitute a hazard to the membership. To a large extent, these are likenesses of United States presidents, American and foreign statesmen, lawyers, writers, poets, educators, scientists, clergymen, and other men and women who in some way have enriched the history of New England or the nation.

Probably the most notorious art treasures ever owned by the Athenaeum were the "Unfinished Heads" of Martha and George Washington, painted from life by Gilbert Stuart in 1796 at Germantown, near Philadelphia. They were commissioned by Martha to hang at Mount Vernon, but Stuart, sensing the monetary advantages of painting copies, simply dawdled and dawdled, saying the portraits were not finished, which of course was true. At last, so the story goes, Martha consented to accept copies instead.13

In 1851, the Athenaeum, aided by public donations, purchased the originals from the artist's widow for fifteen hundred dollars. In the 1870s, they were loaned to the MFA, where they remained in safety for over a century.

In 1979, the Smithsonian Institution suddenly offered the Athenaeum five million dollars for the pair! Bostonians were devastated. However, in 1980 a compromise was reached: for three-year periods, the paintings would hang alternately in Washington and Boston, while the library would receive a satisfactory sum. When Stuart died in Boston in 1828, he had painted five presidents.14

Before the 1970s, this library's great wealth of research material, oriented especially toward biographies and local history, was accessible to serious scholars, and only its art gallery was unreservedly shared with the general public. Today, however, an increasing number of nonmembers are invited to use the bookshelves and reading rooms, and escorted tours are possible on certain days of each week.

From its inception until 1965, when a small bronze plaque was allowed near the front entrance to acknowledge that the Athenaeum building had been declared a national historic landmark, the library was identified only as 10½ Beacon.

Notes

COLONIAL PERIOD (PP. 3–38)

1. Historians disagree on Cabot's probable landfall in North America.
2. *Some Events of Boston and Its Neighbors* (Boston: Walton Advertising and Printing Co. for State Street Trust Co., 1917).
3. Smith probably referred to Potosi, high in the Bolivian Andes, where a huge lode of silver was discovered about 1545.
4. In 1615, while sailing to England, Smith was captured by a French cruiser and imprisoned. During his confinement, he wrote his book on New England.
5. *The Founding Fathers: John Adams, A Biography in His Own Words,* ed. by James Bishop Peabody (New York: Newsweek, 1973), vol. 2, p. 306.
6. *The Founding Fathers: George Washington, A Biography in His Own Words,* ed. by Ralph K. Andrist (New York: Newsweek, 1972), vol. 2, p. 308.
7. Governor Winthrop's oil portrait, which is currently preserved at the AAS, is thought to have been painted in England just before the Puritan migration began; at least, the painting is known to have been in Boston in 1691. Winthrop's journal is now preserved at the MHS.
8. Skilled artisans were essential in the colonies, where they commanded high fees; often they fared better than fishermen and farmers. They certainly enjoyed a higher living standard than their counterparts in England.
9. In 1631, the general court granted Governor Winthrop six hundred acres for a farm in Mystic that he called Ten Hills. A 1637 map of Winthrop's farm is preserved at the MHS.
10. Winthrop, with several others, walked twenty miles through the woodlands from Salem to Charlestown.
11. In mid-October 1985, a group of New England archaeologists unearthed a twenty-foot by forty-foot slate-slab cellar hole in City Square, Charlestown. Historians have long believed this half-acre tract to be the site of Gov. John Winthrop's Great House, where the Massachusetts Bay colony called its meetings in the early 1630s.

Later, the house became a tavern, but during the Battle of Bunker Hill it was firebombed into oblivion by His Majesty's warships standing in the Charles and by General Burgoyne's cannon stationed on the brow of Copp's Hill.

From this ancient foundation and its peripheral trash pits, the 1985 explorers gathered many artifacts before winter settled in. Included were broken tankards, clay pipes, wooden utensils, pieces of eight, part of a leaded window, many oyster shells, traces of a wine cellar, and other suggestions of tavern life—all of which seem to support the conclusions of the diggers: the remains of Great House had come to light.

12. In 1711, Queen Anne claimed first choice of all New England white pines measuring over two feet in diameter found in provincial forests. These were reserved for the masting of her navy.

13. When the Great Elm died in 1876, this ancient tree, which may have shaded Blackstone and his cattle, had a girth of twenty-four feet.

14. Earlier that same year, on February 22, after an American colonial agent, Benjamin Franklin, had addressed the House of Commons, he sent off a hurried letter to his wife, Deborah, in Philadelphia, which ended, "I am well; 'tis all I can say at present except that I am just made happy by a vote in the Commons for the repeal of the Stamp Act" (*Benjamin Franklin: A Biography in His Own Words,* ed. by Thomas Fleming [New York: Newsweek, 1972], vol. 1, pp. 204–5).

15. "Boston Common—Three Pictures," *The Poetical Works of Oliver Wendell Holmes* (Boston and New York: Houghton Mifflin, 1890), p. 151.

16. Mary Caroline Crawford, *Old Boston Days and Ways* (Boston: Little, Brown, 1909), p. 339.

17. *Memorial History of Boston,* ed. by Justin Winsor (Boston: James R. Osgood Co., 1880–1881), vol. 3, p. 252.

18. Excellent examples of Hull's and Sanderson's silver creations may be seen at the MFA and at Yale University. Their coins continued to be minted until Hull's death in 1683. All were dated 1652.

19. Hull owned considerable farmland in New England, especially in Rhode Island; there he bred horses near Point Judith, which he named for his wife.

20. Sewall's own record reveals the dowry as 500 pounds which, according to the editors of an 1875 AAS publication of Hull's diaries, would translate into 10,000 shillings, weighing 125 pounds. Following their marriage, the young couple joined the Hulls in a house that today would stand on Washington Street a little south of Summer Street, and there the Sewalls lived out the remainder of their lives.

21. Soon after his confinement, Sir Edmund tried to escape by wearing a woman's clothes. He passed two guards undetected but a third noticed that the governor had failed to change his shoes.
22. Mather snubbed him.
23. A 1729 Portrait of Sewall by John Smibert hangs at the MFA.
24. Paddock, a loyalist, returned to England with General Gage in 1775.
25. A portrait of Increase Mather painted in London in 1688 is preserved at the MHS. During his later years, Increase served as President of Harvard College.
26. Violent opposition to Cotton Mather's experiment was shown by other clergymen and by extremists who attempted to firebomb his home. Cotton's portrait by Peter Pelham is preserved at the AAS. Pelham's famous mezzotints of "Cottonus Matherus" are thought to be the first of such prints to be made in America.
27. Among others who also searched for the wreck was John Hull, the mintmaster, who sent his ship, *Endeavor,* under the command of Captain Roots.

    In November 1978, having uncovered a missing logbook of the 1687 expedition which pinpointed the wreck's location, a diving team headed by treasure hunter Bert B. Webber of Annsville, Pennsylvania, also explored the ancient reef. The wreck was found and modern salvage operations were begun.
28. According to Cotton Mather, Sir William was the son of James Phips, a blacksmith or a gunsmith, and one of twenty-five children born to the same mother. His portrait, attributed to Thomas Child, hangs at the MFA.
29. "Grandmother's Story of Bunker Hill Battle, *The Poetical Works of Oliver Wendell Holmes,* p. 301.
30. Admiral Graves had been authorized to burn Charlestown to rid it of snipers.

    Legend says that in the spring—as the rebuilding of Charlestown began—skilled fence viewers, restoring old property lines, were greatly aided by the sprouting of peonies, rhubarb, and other perennial plants.
31. Mather's thousand-volume library of rare books was rescued from the great 1676 fire only to be lost in the firebombing of Charlestown on June 17, 1775.
32. Apollos Rivoire reached Boston in 1716 and was apprenticed to John Coney, a goldsmith, who earlier had trained under John Hull, the mintmaster.

33. Joseph Warren Revere studied metallurgy in Europe and expanded the family's copper mills in Canton, Mass.
34. Revere's nineteenth bell, cast in 1797 for the town of Essex, Mass., contains gold and silver donated by the town's parishioners.
35. Page Smith, *John Adams, 1735–1784* (Garden City, N.Y.: Doubleday, 1962), p. 176.
36. Legend says that when Benjamin Franklin was appointed deputy postmaster in 1753, he traveled the Boston Post Road into New England in his chaise, visiting post offices and using his invention, the odometer, to mark the miles. At each mark, so the story goes, a milestone was set and some "Franklinstones" are still extant.

    Franklin later showed that mail on packet boats to Europe could be speeded up if the boats rode the Gulf Stream.
37. A portrait of Colonel Brattle by Copley hangs at the public library in Brattleboro, Vt.; his gambrel-roofed house still stands on Brattle Street in Cambridge.
38. Robert Athearn, *American Heritage History of the United States* (New York, Fawcett, 1971), vol. 3, p. 185.

PROVINCIAL PERIOD (PP. 43–90)

1. By 1708, Boston and Charlestown combined had seventy-eight wharves.
2. Gerrit Schipper's pastel profile of Thomas at age fifty-five is preserved at the AAS.
3. The French, having had quite enough of monarchs, insisted that Philippe spell his title with a small "k." Following his abdication, Philippe lived in England, where tradition suggests that he introduced the fashion of carrying a folded umbrella everywhere.
4. This landing of British troops nearly aroused the countryside to arms. Rebels were ready to ignite the tar bucket on Beacon Hill, but an informer told Governor Bernard, who sent the sheriff to stop them.
5. *The Founding Fathers: John Adams, A Biography in His Own Words,* ed. by James Bishop Peabody (New York: Newsweek, 1973), vol. 1, p. 115.
6. During the Indian Wars, Gage and Washington had served together under General Braddock and had been good friends. Gage married an American woman in 1758.
7. A bronze statue of Anne Hutchinson by Cyrus Dallin stands on the New State House grounds today.

8. On May 31, 1708, diarist Samuel Sewall wrote, "Mr. Crease removes to his new shop next Mr. Sargent's: nothing now to be seen in his former empty place." Thus Sewall suggests that Crease owned the wood-framed house only briefly before the great 1711 fire of October 2 and 3 destroyed it.

9. A banneret weather vane still turning above the cupola is thought to be an old one; some think its workmanship suggests Shem Drowne. (Bannerets are sometimes rudely called "flying pantaloons.")

10. *The Founding Fathers: John Adams, A Biography in His Own Words,* ed. by James Bishop Peabody (New York: Newsweek, 1973), vol. 1, pp. 54–55.

11. Thomas Crafts, whose colorful portrait is preserved at the MHS, was a colonel in the militia and earlier a member of the Tea Party and the Sons of Liberty.

12. Thomas Ball's famous bronze of Washington astride his horse still stands in the Boston Public Garden.

13. John Hancock, first governor of the Commonwealth of Massachusetts, was inaugurated here in 1780. His portrait as a young man, by Copley, may be seen at the MFA.

   Continuing his tour of the States, Washington sat for two hours in Portsmouth, New Hampshire, for artist Christian Gulagher, who painted the President's portrait. This likeness, which many thought was a good one, is now preserved at the MHS. Only a little earlier, the artist had furtively made a pencil sketch of the president while both were seated in King's Chapel.

14. A portrait of Dawes may be seen today at the Cary Memorial Library in Lexington.

15. Franklin was fifteenth among seventeen children.

16. Diarist Samuel Sewall, writing about early unheated churches, remarked, "The Communion bread was frozen pretty hard and rattled in the plates." Some parishioners brought along their dogs to help warm their feet—an idea that quickly spread; but since it encouraged fierce dog fights, it had to be ruled out by the Brethren. Puritan laws also required that taverns and inns empty their houses of all persons near enough and well enough to attend church on Sunday. When people dozed in their pews, they could expect to be prodded by an officer holding a long wand.

17. Bradford's manuscript is now preserved at the Massachusetts State Library.

18. Only minutes after the march 6 meeting at Old South, Samuel Adams and others met with Governor Hutchinson at Old State House to

present their demands for a withdrawal of all British troops from the town. Copley's famous portrait depicts Adams pointing to the Province of Massachusetts Bay Charter as proof that Hutchinson had the power to take this action. This painting was commissioned by John Hancock in 1772. Edward Truman's portrait of Hutchinson at about age thirty is now owned by the MHS.

19. Although loyal to his king, Hutchinson believed Parliament's tax measures in the colonies were unwise.

20. Page Smith, *John Adams, 1735–1784* (Garden City, N.Y.: Doubleday, 1962), p. 147.

21. A fourth cargo ship, the *William,* carrying tea and three hundred whale oil lamps for Boston streets, never arrived at Griffin's Wharf. It was wrecked on a Cape Cod shore, but its cargo was salvaged.

22. *The Founding Fathers: John Adams, A Biography in His Own Words,* ed. by James Bishop Peabody, vol. 1, p. 140.

23. Boston ladies diligently brewed "Liberty Tea" from sage, loosestrife, and other herbs.

24. Gage was no stranger to Americans, having served with them under General Braddock during the French and Indian Wars. In 1763, he had taken over (from Jeffrey Amherst) as commander of all North American forces. His portrait by Copley hangs at New State House today.

25. Page Smith, *John Adams, p.* 161.

26. Portraits of John Adams in Boston and nearby towns: pastels of John and Abigail by Benjamin Blythe, the MHS; a 1783 oil by Copley, Harvard University; a 1788 oil by Mather Brown, the Boston Athenaeum; an oil by John Trumbull, the Fogg Museum; a marble bust by J. B. Binon, the Athenaeum; and an oil by Gilbert Stuart, Adams Mansion.

27. Symbols of ancient Rome were growing in popularity at that time and Warren had draped himself in a Roman toga for the occasion.

28. Today, a colorful portrait of Peter Faneuil by John Smibert hangs at the MHS, and the Faneuil family monument may still be seen in the southwest corner of Old Granary.

29. Mary Williams, one of the well-to-do Bostonians painted by Smibert, later became his wife. Her portrait hangs at the MHS.

   Smibert, who began his career as a house painter, studied art in London and Italy. He arrived at Newport, R.I., with a group of educators in early 1729 and painted briefly there before setting up a studio in Boston. One of his earliest Newport paintings, now at Yale, shows nine Bermuda Group educators, including himself.

In the mid-1740s, at Smibert's studio on Queen Street (now Court Street), an eager eight-year-old boy watched the artist at work—his name, John Singleton Copley.

30. The 16' × 30' painting by George Healy, which dominates the west end of the second-floor meeting hall, depicts Daniel Webster speaking before the U.S. Senate. It was commissioned by Louis Philippe, the French king who, as a young duke, had lived near Faneuil Hall for a time. (See narrative for Capen House in this work.)

31. *Some Events of Boston and Its Neighbors* (Boston: Walton Advertising and Printing Co. for State Street Trust Co., 1917), p. 17.

32. The original marble sculpture by Ann Whitney now stands in the rotunda of the Capitol in Washington, D.C.

33. During Andros's first three months in Boston, Anglican services were conducted for him in the first Town House library.

34. Sir Henry, a lineal descendant of Oliver Cromwell, caused quite a stir in Boston over a long affair that eventually ended in his marriage to Agnes Surriage, a lovely Marblehead tavern girl.

35. By early March 1770, all the Townshend Acts had been repealed except the tax on tea.

36. When New Hampshire's colonial governor, John Wentworth, learned of this attack, he called it "high treason." But soon he was forced to flee to safety within fortified Boston. Copley's 1769 oil portrait of Wentworth hangs in the Hood Museum of Art, Dartmouth College.

37. About a month earlier, this colorful soldier and farmer had left his plow in its furrow to heed the Lexington alarm. Trumbull's pencil portrait of Putnam now hangs at the Wadsworth Atheneum Museum of Art in Hartford.

    On the night of the redcoats' tormented thirty-mile retreat from Concord and Lexington, General Gage ordered a redoubt to be raised on Breed's Hill to protect his exhausted regulars returning by way of Charlestown Neck. By the next afternoon, however, both the hill and Charlestown had been abandoned.

38. The names, Bunker Hill and Breed's Hill, have long been used interchangeably; the battle is usually called Bunker, although the location is Breed's, which of course only adds to the confusion.

39. Red had been the accepted color for British military uniforms for about a century; it continued so until 1914.

40. At one point, the militia was so short of ammunition that a bounty was offered for turning in spent British balls. But that was soon stopped:

eager militiamen died trying to catch enemy balls as they bounced along the ground.

41. This Congress also authorized an issue of Continental currency and established a United Colonies Post Office under the direction of Benjamin Franklin.

42. Washington refused to accept payment for his services. By his marriage to Martha Custis in 1759, he had become a wealthy man. The Washington Elm on Cambridge Common survived until 1923.

43. Washington's first intelligence of the Breed's Hill action was received in New York, where he intercepted a fast courier on his way to Philadelphia.

44. Many owners of large tobacco plantations and other tidewater farm operations along the middle and southern Atlantic seaboard were reluctant to embrace rebel attitudes toward independence. Theirs was a different society, with essentially only two classes: aristocrats and slaves. Shipowners and merchants could sail directly from London to the private dock of a plantation owner. Moreover, business was excellent.

45. Washington wrote his brother, John Augustine, that the Breed's Hill battle had cost the British 1,043, lives, while the defenders had lost 138.

46. John Bartlett, *Familiar Quotations* (Boston: Little, Brown, 1955), p. 353.

47. When seized by the Americans in 1776, Dorchester Heights had two peaks about equal in height.

48. A portrait of Rufus Putnam now hangs at Independence National Historic Park in Philadelphia.

49. Earlier, Knox, whose London Bookstore stood just south of the Old State House, had witnessed the Boston Massacre and had served at Bunker Hill as a volunteer. Later, he would direct Washington's bold Christmas night crossing of the ice-choked Delaware during which, according to legend, the chief jokingly shouted to his three hundred-pound colonel, "Shift your back sides, Knox, or we'll all be upset." Still later, the president would appoint him secretary of war.

50. Natalie S. Bobar, *Abigail Adams: Witness to a Revolution* (Athenium Books for Young Readers/Simon and Schuster, 1995), p. 68.

51. Gilbert Stuart's canvas of Washington at Dorchester Heights was painted seven years after the general's death. It was commissioned to hang at Faneuil Hall but currently it hangs at the MFA, while a copy by Stuart's daughter hangs at Faneuil Hall.

52. The Boston Neck fortification stood near what is now the intersection of Washington and Dover Streets.

53. Many historians believe that even before Dorchester Heights, Howe's

plans to quit the town were well underway; they reason that after the battles of April and June 1775, available British forces were never strong enough to break through the siege with any lasting success.

54. *The Founding Fathers: George Washington, A Biography in His Own Words,* ed. by Ralph K. Andrist (New York: Newsweek, 1972), vol. 1, p. 125.

55. Page Smith, *John Adams, 1735–1784* (Garden City, N.Y.: Doubleday, 1962), vol. 1, pp. 252–253.

FEDERAL PERIOD (PP. 96–126)

1. Quoted in a letter written by Abigail Adams, *The Founding Fathers: John Adams, A Biography in His Own Words,* ed. by James Bishop Peabody (New York: Newsweek, 1973), vol. 2, p. 370.

2. Among those New England merchants who bartered with the Oregon Indians for furs to carry to Canton was Capt. Robert Gray of Boston. Near the trading site, Gray discovered a great river which he named after the *Columbia,* one of America's first trading ships to circumnavigate the globe.

3. American sea captains who engaged in the oriental trade were indebted to the calculations of New England's navigator and astronomer, Nathaniel Bowditch, who first published his *New American Practical Navigator* in 1802—thus correcting about eight thousand errors in the *1799 Practical Navigator* published by Moore.

4. Alice G. B. Lockwood, ed., *Gardens of Colony and State* (New York: Charles Scribner's Sons, 1931), 1:32. Two oil portraits of Thomas Hancock are still extant. The first, by John Smibert, painted when Thomas was a young man, hangs at the MFA. The second, by Copley, now a part of the Harvard Collection, shows the merchant at about sixty.

5. A portrait of Lord Percy may be seen at the Cary Memorial Library in Lexington.

6. *Memorial History of Boston,* ed. by Justin Winsor (Boston: James R. Osgood Co., 1880–1881), vol. 3, p. 70.

7. A pastel self-portrait of Copley as a young man hangs at the Winterthur Museum in Wilmington, Delaware.

8. Susan and Michael Southworth, *AIA Guide to Boston* (Guilford, Conn.: Globe Pequot Press, 1992), p. 177.

9. Although Dallin's original sculpture of Revere was chosen the winner of an 1884 competition for a statue to stand in Copley Square, delay followed delay; the bronze was not placed in its present location until 1940.

10. A colorful Lafayette portrait by Joseph Boze hangs at the MHS. It was painted for Thomas Jefferson while he was minister to France in the 1780s. Another Lafayette likeness by Phalipon hangs at Old State House.

11. Gilbert Stuart's portrait of John Adams, painted in Quincy about this time, now hanging at Adams Mansion, is probably a good likeness of the man with whom Lafayette dined. Adams told Mayor Quincy that he liked to sit for Stuart, "for he lets me do just what I please and keeps me constantly amused by his conversation" (*John Adams, A Biography in His Own Words,* pp. 405–6).

12. Governor Winthrop simply dawdled about returning the charter and meanwhile, as England's conflict with Scotland grew stronger, the whole matter of returning the document was shelved.

13. Castle Island is the oldest military base in continuous use in the United States. From 1686 to 1776, it was manned mostly by British officers and men. In 1799, President Adams renamed it Fort Independence.

GREEK REVIVAL PERIOD (PP. 133–158)

1. Houdon's bust of Jefferson may be seen at the MFA.

2. President Monroe appointed Charles Bulfinch to oversee the restoration of the Capitol.

3. A portrait of Nicholas Biddle by Sully hangs at Andalusia today.

4. Although as early as 1775 General Braddock's army had used Conestoga-type freight wagons which went anywhere, road systems leading westward were slow in developing. Before 1793 for example, nothing better than a horse trail had joined the Connecticut Valley settlements to Albany.

5. Laommi Baldwin, who planned and engineered the Middlesex Canal, also introduced the elegant Baldwin apple. Tradition says discovery of his famous apple was accidental. One day while surveying, he noticed that woodpeckers preferred the fruit of one wild apple tree above all others; after tasting the apple himself, he cut many scions for grafting.

6. A barge canal still operates westward from the Hudson.

7. At last at 10 A.M. September 3, Benjamin Franklin, John Adams, and John Jay formally signed the final treaty in Paris with John Hartly, a representative of George III. But not until January 14, 1784, did Congress ratify the signing.

8. President Washington laid the cornerstone for the Capitol in 1793. Earlier, he had chosen the site for the District of Columbia.

9. Bulfinch's likeness, painted in London by the American artist Mather Brown when Charles was in his early twenties, is now a part of the Harvard Collection.

10. On April 16, 1789, Washington wrote in his diary: "About ten o'clock I bade adieu to Mount Vernon, to private life, and to domestic felicity; and, with a mind oppressed with more anxious and painful sensations than I have words to express, set out for New York" (*Founding Fathers: George Washington, A Biography in His Own Words*, vol. 2, p. 295).

11. A bronze likeness of Mayor Quincy by Thomas Ball stands before Old City Hall. From 1805 to 1883, Quincy served in the U.S. Congress. As a Federalist, however, he resigned in opposition to the War of 1812. His marble bust by Thomas Crawford stands at the Boston Athenaeum.

12. Baked Indian pudding, made from ground native corn and tasty West Indian molasses, was a delicacy relished around all early–New England firesides.

13. Stuart, although prolific, often procrastinated. In 1815, in Boston, he completed a portrait of Abigail Adams, wife of the second president, that he had begun in 1800. This painting now hangs in the National Gallery of Art.

14. John Savage's 1790 portraits of George and Martha, painted for John Adams, still hang at Adams Mansion in Quincy.

Bibliography

The reading sources listed here were invaluable in constructing the narratives of this work.

Adams, Charles Francis. *Familiar Letters of John and his wife Abigail Adams during the Revolution.* Cambridge, Mass.: Riverside Press, 1876.

Amory, Mary Babcock. *The Domestic and Artistic Life of John Singleton Copley, R.A.* Boston: Houghton Mifflin, 1882.

Andrews, Wayne. *Architecture in New England.* Brattleboro, Vt.: Steven Green Press, 1973.

Athearn, Robert G. *American Heritage History of the United States.* 6 vols. New York: Fawcett Publications, 1971.

Andrist, Ralph K., ed. *The Founding Fathers: George Washington, A Biography in His Own Words.* Vol. 2. New York: Newsweek, 1972.

Artist in America, The. Compiled by the editors of *Art in America.* New York: Norton, 1967.

Barquest, David. "John Trumbull's American History Paintings." *Art and Antiques Magazine,* November–December, 1982.

Bellows, Robert P. "Some Boston Weathervanes." Unpublished manuscript, author's collection, ca. 1952.

Bobar, Natalie S., *Abigail Adams: Witness to a Revolution.* New York: Atheneum Books for Young Readers/Simon and Schuster, 1995.

Bradford, William. *Of Plymouth Plantation.* Edited by Harvey Wish. New York: Capricorn Books, 1962.

Brereton, John. *The Discovery of the North Part of Virginia.* London: George Bishop, 1602. Ann Arbor: Great Americana, Readex Micro Print, 1966.

Bridgwater, William, and Elizabeth J. Sherwood, eds. *The Columbia Encyclopedia.* 2d ed. New York: Columbia University Press, 1956.

British Library. *The American War of Independence 1775–1783.* London: British Museum Publications, 1975.

Bulfinch, Ellen S. *The Life and Letters of Charles Bulfinch, Architect.* Boston: Houghton Mifflin, 1896.

Bunting, W. H. *Portrait of a Port, Boston 1852–1914.* Cambridge, Mass.: Harvard University Press, 1971.

Chase, Sarah B. "A Brief Survey of the Architectural History of Old State House, Boston, Massachusetts." *S.P.N.E.A. Bulletin* 68 (1978). (Society for the Preservation of New England Antiquities.)

Chidsley, Donald Barr. "The Old Boston Post Roads." *National Geographic Magazine,* August 1962.

Clark, David L. *The Old North Church.* Everett, Mass.: Acme Printing Co.

Crawford, Mary Caroline. *Old Boston Days and Ways.* Little, Brown, 1909.

Crossman, Carl O. *The China Trade: Export Paintings, Furniture, Silver, and Other Objects.* Princeton: Pine Press, 1972.

Cummings, Abbott Lowell. *The Framed Houses of Massachusetts Bay.* Cambridge, Mass.: Harvard University Press, 1979.

Cunliff, Marcus. "How Independence was Signed, Sealed, and then Delivered." *Smithsonian Magazine,* August 1983.

Deitz, Paula. "The First American Landscape." *Connoisseur Magazine,* December 1982.

DePauw, Linda Grant, and Conover Hunt. *Remember the Ladies.* New York: Viking Press, 1976.

Detwiller, Frederic C. "The Evolution of Shirley-Eustis House." *S.P.N.E.A. Bulletin* 70 (1980).

Drake, Samuel Adams. *Old Landmarks and Historic Personages of Boston.* Boston: James Osgood, 1873.

Earle, Alice Morse. *Home Life in Colonial Days: Customs and Fashions in Old New England.* New York: Macmillan, 1899.

Eberlein, Harold Donaldson. *190 High Street, the Home of Washington and Adams, 1790–1800.* Philadelphia: American Philosophical Society, 1953.

Farnsworth, Clyde H. "Future King Sampled U.S. Life in 1797." *New York Times,* 20 July 1976.

Fleming, Thomas, ed. *The Founding Fathers: Benjamin Franklin, a Biography in His Own Words,* vol. 1. New York: Newsweek, 1972.

Flexnor, James T., and Linda B. Samter. *The Face of Liberty.* New York: C. N. Potter, Inc., 1972.

Forbes, Allan, and Paul F. Codman. *France and New England.* 3 vols. Boston: State Street Trust Co., 1925–1927.

Forbes, Esther. *Paul Revere and the World He Lived In.* Boston: Houghton Mifflin, 1942.

Gardener, Joseph L., ed. *The Founding Fathers: Washington, a Biography in His Own Words,* vol. 1. New York: Newsweek, 1972.

Garrett, Wendell. (Editorial about the Boston Athenaeum.) *Antiques Magazine,* June 1973.

Grunwald, Henry A. "Independence." *Time Magazine,* 4 July 1775, special issue.

Halsey, Thomas, ed. *The Diary of Samuel Sewall.* 2 vols. New York: Farrar, Straus, and Giroux, 1973.

Hamlin, Talbot. *Greek Revival Architecture in America.* Oxford: Oxford University Press, 1944.

Harris, John, ed. "Boston Tea Party," *Boston Globe,* 1975.

——. "Battle of Bunker Hill," *Boston Globe,* 1975.

——. "Lexington and Concord Alarm," *Boston Globe,* 1975.

Hill, Douglas. *The English to New England.* New York: C. N. Potter, Inc., 1975.

Holmes, Oliver Wendell. *The Poetical Works of Oliver Wendell Holmes.* Cambridge, Mass.: Riverside Press, 1890.

Hutchinson, Thomas. *History of the Colony and Province of Massachusetts Bay.* Ed. by Lawrence Shaw Mayo. 3 vols. Cambridge, Mass.: Harvard University Press, 1936.

Jensen, Albert C. "The Cod: A Case of Supervised Neglect." *Natural History Magazine,* December 1973.

Jones, Howard Mumford, and Zabau Besse, eds. *The Many Voices of Boston.* Boston: Atlantic–Little, Brown and Co., 1975.

Kales, Emily, and David Kales. *All about Boston Harbor Islands.* Boston: Herman Publishing Co., 1976.

Kilham, Walter. *Boston After Bulfinch.* Cambridge, Mass.: Harvard University Press, 1946.

Lathrop, Elise. *Historic Houses of Early America.* New York: Tudor Publishing, 1927.

Lincoln, Edith Morse. Legend about Otis's gold doubloons. Unpublished manuscript in author's collection.

Lockwood, Alice G. B. *Gardens of Colony and State.* New York: Charles Scribner's Sons, 1931.

Longfellow, Henry W. "Paul Revere's Ride." *The Poetical Works of Henry Wadsworth Longfellow.* Boston: Houghton Mifflin, 1882.

MacDonald, E. *Old Copp's Hill and Burial Ground.* Boston: published by the author, 1882.

Mackay, Robert. "Cast-iron architecture on Beacon Hill in Boston." *Antiques Magazine,* June 1975.

McKetcham, Richard. *Decisive Day.* New York: Doubleday, 1975.

Morgunroth, Lynda. "Paul Revere, Portrait of a Family Man." *Boston Globe,* April 1983.

Morris, Richard B., ed. *Encyclopedia of American History.* New York: Harper and Brothers, 1953.

Morrison, Samuel Eliot. *The Maritime History of Massachusetts.* Boston: Houghton Mifflin, 1941.

——. *Builders of the Bay Colony.* Boston: Houghton Mifflin, 1958.

——. *The European Discovery of America: The Northern Voyages.* Oxford: Oxford University Press, 1971.

Museum of Fine Arts. *Paul Revere's Boston, 1735–1818.* Boston: Museum of Fine Arts, 1975.

National Maritime Museum. *1776: The British Story of the American Revolution.* London: Times Newspapers, 1976.

Palfrey, John Gorham. *Palfrey's History of New England.* Boston: Little, Brown, 1859.

Palladio, Andrea. *The Four Books of Architecture.* 4 vols. Reprint. New York: Dover Publishing, 1965.

Palmer, Arlene. *A Winterthur Guide to Chinese Export Porcelain.* New York: Crown Publishers, 1976.

Peabody, James B., ed. *The Founding Fathers: John Adams, A Biography in His Own Words.* vols. 1 and 2. New York: Newsweek, 1973.

Pearson, Danella. "Shirley-Eustis House Landscape History." Boston: *S.P.N.E.A. Bulletin,* vol. 70 (1980).

Pendery, Steven. "Charlestown gets in its (historic) digs." *Boston Herald,* 1 December 1985.

Pickering, Ernest. *The Homes of America.* New York: Bramhall House, 1976.

Richmond, Robert P. *Powder Alarm 1774.* Princeton: Auerbach Publishers, 1971.

Robinson, William S. *Abandoned New England.* Boston: Little, Brown, 1976.

Ross, Marjorie Drake. *The Book of Boston: The Colonial Period.* New York: Hastings House Publishers, 1960.

——. *The Book of Boston: The Federal Period.* New York: Hastings House Publishers, 1961.

Smith, Page. *John Adams.* 2 vols. New York: Doubleday, 1962.

Some Events of Boston and Its Neighbors. Boston: State Street Trust Co., 1917.

Southworth, Susan. *AIA Guide to Boston.* Guilford, Conn.: Globe Pequot Press, 1992.

Stark, James H. *Stark's Antique Views of Ye Towne of Boston.* Boston: Morse-Purce Co., 1907.

Tourtelot, Arthur Bernon. *Benjamin Franklin: The Shaping of Genius, The Boston Years.* Garden City, N.Y.: Doubleday, 1977.

Thwing, Annie H. *The Crooked and Narrow Streets of the Town of Boston, 1630–1822.* Boston: Charles E. Lariat Co., 1930.

Wagenchneght, Edward. *A Pictorial History of New England.* New York: Crown, 1976.

Washington Star. (Sale of Boston Atheneum Portraits of George and Martha Washington.) *New York Times,* 8 February 1980.

Webster, Mary Phillips, and Charles F. Morris. *The Story of the Suffolk Resolves.* Milton, Mass.: Milton, Massachusetts Historical Commission, 1973.

Wertenbaker, Thomas J. *The First Americans, 1607–1690.* New York: Macmillan, 1927.

Weston, George F., Jr. *Boston Ways, High, By, and Folk.* Boston: Beacon Press, 1957.

Whitehall, Walter. "Portrait busts in the library of the Boston Athenaeum." *Antiques Magazine,* June 1973.

Wilford, John Noble. "Prints of Franklin's Gulf Stream Found." *New York Times,* 8 February 1980.

Winn, Robert M. "A Guide at a Glance" of Historic Boston. Wollaston, Mass.: n.p., 1947.

Winsor, Justin, ed. *Memorial History of Boston.* 4 vols. Boston: James R. Osgood Co., 1880–1881.

Winthrop, John. *History of New England.* Boston: Phelps and Farnham, 1825.

Acknowledgments

The following New England museums and libraries were very helpful in researching this work:

Bridge Memorial Library of Walpole, N.H.

Rockingham Public Library of Bellows Falls, Vt.

Museum of Fine Arts, Boston; Bostonian Society; Society for the Preservation of New England Antiquities (S.P.N.E.A.); Reference Library, Boston Public Library; Boston Anthaeum; Concord Antiquarian Society; Peabody Museum of Salem; Essex Institute of Salem; Old Sturbridge Village Museum; Museum of the American China Trade in Salem; Museum of Our National Heritage in Lexington; Massachusetts Historical Society; Memorial Hall Museum in Deerfield, Mass.

Wadsworth Atheneum Museum of Art in Hartford, Conn.

I am especially grateful for the help of four manuscript readers who, from their already busy lives, have applied their training, patience, and encouragement toward the completion of this work: Geraldine Biddle, Marion Andros, Dr. William Tatem, and Bertha Gleason.